MARTIN LUTHER
as He Lived and Breathed

CASCADE COMPANIONS

The Christian theological tradition provides an embarrassment of riches: from scripture to modern scholarship, we are blessed with a vast and complex theological inheritance. And yet this feast of traditional riches is too frequently inaccessible to the general reader.

The Cascade Companions series addresses the challenge by publishing books that combine academic rigor with broad appeal and readability. They aim to introduce nonspecialist readers to that vital storehouse of authors, documents, themes, histories, arguments, and movements that comprise this heritage with brief yet compelling volumes.

TITLES IN THIS SERIES:

Reading Augustine by Jason Byassee
Conflict, Community, and Honor by John H. Elliott
An Introduction to the Desert Fathers by Jason Byassee
Reading Paul by Michael J. Gorman
Theology and Culture by D. Stephen Long
Creation and Evolution by Tatha Wiley
Theological Interpretation of Scripture by Stephen Fowl
Reading Bonhoeffer by Geffrey B. Kelly
Justpeace Ethics by Jarem Sawatsky
Feminism and Christianity by Caryn D. Griswold
Angels, Worms, and Bogeys by Michelle A. Clifton-Soderstrom
Christianity and Politics by C. C. Pecknold
A Way to Scholasticism by Peter S. Dillard
Theological Theodicy by Daniel Castelo
The Letter to the Hebrews in Social-Scientific Perspective by David A. deSilva
Basil of Caesarea by Andrew Radde-Galwitz
A Guide to St. Symeon the New Theologian by Hannah Hunt
Reading John by Christopher W. Skinner

MARTIN LUTHER
as He Lived and Breathed

Recollections of the Reformer

ROBERT KOLB

 CASCADE *Books* · Eugene, Oregon

MARTIN LUTHER AS HE LIVED AND BREATHED
Recollections of the Reformer

Cascade Companions

Copyright © 2018 Robert Kolb. All rights reserved. Except for brief quotations in critical publications or reviews, no part of this book may be reproduced in any manner without prior written permission from the publisher. Write: Permissions, Wipf and Stock Publishers, 199 W. 8th Ave., Suite 3, Eugene, OR 97401.

Cascade Books
An Imprint of Wipf and Stock Publishers
199 W. 8th Ave., Suite 3
Eugene, OR 97401

www.wipfandstock.com

PAPERBACK ISBN: 978-1-62564-778-8
HARDCOVER ISBN: 978-1-4982-8693-0
EBOOK ISBN: 978-1-5326-5947-8

Cataloging-in-Publication data:

Names: Kolb, Robert, 1941–, author.

Title: Martin Luther as he lived and breathed : recollections of the reformer / Robert Kolb.

Description: Eugene, OR: Cascade Books, 2018. | Cascade Companions. | Includes bibliographical references and index.

Identifiers: ISBN: 978-1-62564-778-8 (paperback). | ISBN: 978-1-4982-8693-0 (hardcover). | ISBN: 978-1-5326-5947-8 (epub).

Subjects: LCSH: Luther, Martin, 1483–1546. | Theology, Doctrinal—History—16th centtury.

Classification: BR325 K66 2018 (print). | BR325 (epub).

Manufactured in the U.S.A.

Contents

Introduction: Will the Real Martin Luther
   Please Stand Up? vii

1. The Stations of Childhood and Youth 1
2. The Cloister and Further Studies 18
3. The Maturation of a Theologian 35
4. The Media Revolution and the Thickets of
   Controversy 55
5. Worms, the Wartburg, and Wittenberg 81
6. 1525, a Year of Crises 101
7. The Institutionalization of the Movement 121
8. The New Normal of the 1530s and 1540s 142

Index of Persons 165

Index of Interviews by Person Interviewed 169

Introduction

Will the Real Martin Luther Please Stand Up

GIVEN BOOK PRICES TODAY, it cannot be said that Luther biographies are a dime a dozen, but with two thousand dollars we could easily buy the four- to five-dozen accounts of Luther's life or significant portions of it that are currently available in English. What does this little volume add to all that is gathered in the stack? Mark U. Edwards Jr., author of three of the most helpful focused studies of elements of Luther's career,[1] has observed that we know more about Luther than most of his contemporaries did because we have a great deal more documentary evidence than did nearly all of them.[2] Listening to people who experienced Luther, up close or from afar, helps us gain perspective on this

---

1. Mark U. Edwards Jr., *Luther and the False Brethren* (Stanford: Stanford University Press, 1975); Edwards, *Luther's Last Battles: Politics and Polemics, 1531–46* (Ithaca: Cornell University Press, 1983); Edwards, *Printing, Propaganda, and Martin Luther* (1994; reprint, Minneapolis: Fortress, 2004).

2. Edwards, *Printing and Propaganda*, 4.

personality that divided his contemporaries into those who found in him a liberator and truth-teller like no other and those who deeply feared what they saw as the destruction that he was wreaking on their world.

This overview of Luther's life presents a narrator's brief summary of the main stations of Luther's unfolding preparation for public leadership and his direction of the reform movement that radiated from Wittenberg into many corners of Europe in his time. Accompanying the narrator's recital of the main thread of his story are "interviews," quotations, some from Luther himself, some from his students or followers, some from his critics and enemies. They reveal the perspectives of individuals with a variety of vantage points from which they viewed the Wittenberg reformer. Readers will gain here a series of sixteenth-century perceptions on the man to whom very few were indifferent. Those perceptions reflect both adoring admiration from those who were absorbing his ideas as best they could or wished to and the horrified revulsion of those who reacted to him with fear that his message was bringing the destruction of church and society.

Therefore, rather than offering a fully adequate overview of Luther's life—to say nothing of (the impossible venture of) a complete review of Luther's life, this volume is an invitation to read more in other books. It hopes to lure readers into further exploration of the remarkable personality and teaching of this man who could command the attention of people throughout the world five hundred years after his life.

In the conclusion to his pioneering assessment of the changing views of the reformer from Wittenberg, Horst Stephan observed that the ever-new pictures or images of Luther are always "born out of a new encounter with the testimony of the original image, and they are reflections of

Introduction

his form in water of different depths and different hues."[3] In a degree perhaps unique in the history of the church since the apostolic age, the "image" of this single person, Martin Luther, has directly shaped the institutions and life of a large portion of Christendom. Both his actions and his way of perceiving the world, God, and what it means to be human have influenced the lives of his adherents and also his critics. Indeed, Calvinist churches, for example, have looked to John Calvin as model and magister for their ecclesiastical life. John Wesley has exercised a continuing role in the orientation of Methodist churches. To a far greater extent, however, Lutheran churches have found in Luther not only a teacher but also a prophetic hero and authority. Heinrich Bornkamm's observation extends beyond the borders of the German cultural realm that he was sketching when he wrote, "Every presentation and assessment of Luther and the Reformation means a critical engagement with the foundations of our more recent history. Like no other historical figure, that of Luther always compels anew a comprehensive reflection of the religious, spiritual, and political problems of our lives."[4]

Those "interviewed" in this volume give accounts shaped by their own experiences with the man. Typical is his student and avid supporter Cyriakus Spangenberg. Spangenberg sometimes made what seem like exaggerated claims about the gifts and impact of his teacher's teaching and personality upon him and others. However, it is misleading to say, as did Wolfgang Hermann in his study of Spangenberg's sermons on Luther's person and work, that

---

3. Horst Stephan, *Luther in den Wandlungen seiner Kirche* (Studien zur Geschichte des neueren Protestantismus 1; Giessen: Töpelmann, 1907), 127.

4. Heinrich Bornkamm, *Luther im Spiegel der deutschen Geistesgeschichte* (Heidelberg: Quelle & Meyer, 1955), 11.

Introduction

"the Mansfeld pastor does not present any of his personal impressions of Luther; rather, for him Luther is simply the Saint, to whom only good characteristics may be ascribed, a saint who belongs to a chain of great warriors of God throughout church history and who finally is distinct from everything human."[5] It is indeed regrettable that Spangenberg did not offer more anecdotal material on his personal experiences at Luther's table and lecture hall. Nonetheless, Spangenberg was continually presenting his personal impression of Luther. These impressions convey the sense that this man was larger than life, a prophet of God—indeed, "a saint who belongs to a chain of great warriors of God throughout church history."

In listening to these "interviews" with Spangenberg and his contemporaries, readers must remember that all historical reports depict events and personalities from their own individual perspectives. Twenty-first-century observers of a foreign culture separated from us by five hundred years often fail to remember and perhaps cannot truly appreciate the deep emotions that informed such reports. A prominent clergyman such as Johannes Cochlaeus could not react to Luther in any other way than with deep outrage and a profound sense of betrayal that one of the theologians' guild so threatened public order and the truth of the church. Luther was challenging the concepts of human contribution to a person's standing before God and the pope's place as vicar of Christ. These convictions served to ensure both order within the church and the unity of western Europe for people like Cochlaeus. On the other hand, those who had experienced Luther personally, such as Johannes Mathesius, Cyriacus Spangenberg, and Ludwig Rabus, had felt in the power of his message the fulfillment

5. Wolfgang Herrmann, "Die Lutherpredigten des Cyriacus Spangenberg," *Mansfelder Blätter* 39 (1934/1935) 59 [7–95].

Introduction

of the late medieval hopes for a prophet. Their grandparents and great-grandparents had longed for such a prophet, who would counter the corruption and insecurities of that late medieval world. Luther's students and other disciples had the bitter taste of betrayal by one who claimed to be Christ's vicar and who at the same time not only rejected what they had found to be Christ's teaching in Scripture but also was burning at the stake those who followed that teaching. They were outraged that medieval Catholic theologians who claimed to be "*Doctores in Biblia*"—teachers of the Bible—were defending a system of pastoral care that had proved itself ineffective and downright deceptive.

Both enthusiasm and enmity can twist perceptions of events and readings of documents. Therefore, the readers of this volume will need a grain or two of salt when reading these accounts. There is something there in each individual's reflections on what they have read and heard and experienced personally, but facticity was sometimes sacrificed to feelings. With such feelings Cochlaeus and Mathesius, as well as Luther himself, gave the observations of the events of the Wittenberg Reformation found in this volume. Readers should work as best they can on sorting out what stands behind words of praise and condemnation that reflects aspects of historical reality, recognizing how they themselves also import their own experiences and values into their reading of the sources.

Where possible, material in the interviews is taken from English translations so that readers unable to read German and Latin can look at the fuller context of the citations. Even in these cases, the texts in this volume may differ from those translations since they are based on original texts, in original printings in edited form. Some citations have been altered slightly to fit them into the interview format.

Introduction

The list of those interviewed, in addition to Luther himself, includes:

1) **Georg Benedict** came from his native Lüneburg to study at Wittenberg at the end of the 1510s. Source: Boehmer, Heinrich. *Der junge Luther*, 366-67. 3rd ed. Leipzig: Koehler & Amelang, 1939.

2) **Martin Bucer** *(1491–1551)* heard Luther defend his "theology of the cross" at Heidelberg in 1518. He later became the leader of the church in Strassburg. His efforts to build bridges between Luther and the Swiss reformers, who rejected Luther's understanding of the true presence of Christ's body and blood in the Lord's Supper, ultimately failed. He and Luther reached an agreement in the Wittenberg Concord of 1536. Source: Bucer, Martin. *Correspondance de Martin Bucer*, vol. 1. Edited by Jean Rott et al. 8 vols. Leiden: Brill, 1979.

3) **Johannes Cochlaeus** *(1479–1552)* served at the court of Duke Georg of Saxony and absorbed his prince's antagonism to Georg's despised cousin Frederick the Wise and anything that happened in electoral Saxony. Cochlaeus embodied the fears of adherents of the papacy that Luther was destroying the pillars of stability of their world. He invented the genre of polemical biography and gathered stories about Luther in order to discredit him. Regardless of whether these always correspond to actual facts, they offer a clear depiction of the enmity that Luther's proposals for reform aroused in those who believed in the truth and the necessity of papal governance of church and secular world. Source: Cochlaeus, Johannes. *Historia de actis et scriptis Martini Lutheri Saxonis*, . . . (originally published in 1549). I have used Paris: Guillaume Chauldiere, 1565. ET: *Luther's Lives: Two Contemporary Accounts of Martin Luther*. Translated and annotated by Elizabeth Vandiver et al. Manchester: Manchester University Press, 2002.

Introduction

4) **Veit Dietrich** *(1506-1549)* lived with the Luther family and served as Luther's amanuensis and editor before going to Nuremberg as a parish pastor. Source: WA Br 5: 379, Nr. 1595.

5) **Johannes Hoffmeister** *(1509/1510-1547)* was an Augustinian brother of Luther who strove to build up his order after the decimation experienced as a result of so many of his brothers leaving it to support Luther's call for reform. Source: Volz, Hans, ed. *Drei Schriften gegen Luthers Schmalkaldische Artikel von Cochläus, Witzel und Hoffmeister (1538 und 1539)*. Münster: Aschendorf, 1932.

6) **Johannes Mathesius** *(1504-1565)* studied in Wittenberg at least twice, in 1529 and in 1540, and perhaps for one or two other periods. From his pulpit in Joachimsthal in Bohemia, he preached a series of seventeen sermons on Luther's life and significance, a prime source for contemporary tales and anecdotes about the reformer's life. Source: Mathesius, Johannes. *Historien, Von des Ehrwirdigen in Gott Seligen thewren Manns Gottes, Doctoris Martini Luthers/anfang/lehr/leben vnd sterben* . . . . Nuremberg: Ulrich Neuber, 1566.

7) **Philip Melanchthon** *(1497-1560)* was from 1518 until Luther's death his colleague, conversation partner, teacher, and pupil. Melanchthon and Luther formed a mutually supportive team, feeding on each other's intellectual stimulation and emotional support. Source: Bretschneider, C. G. and H. E. Bindweil, eds. *Philippi Melanthonis Opera quae supersunt omnia*, vol. 6. 28 vols. Corpus Reformatorum. Halle: Schwetschke, 1834-1860. ET: *Luther's Lives: Two Contemporary Accounts of Martin Luther*. Translated and annotated Elizabeth Vandiver et al. Manchester: Manchester University Press, 2002.

8) **Petrus Mosellanus** *(1493-1524)* was an instructor in Leipzig and a recorder of Luther's debate with Johann

Eck in 1519. Mosellanus belonged to the circle of biblical humanists at the University of Leipzig. Source: Hoppe, A. F., ed. *Dr. Martin Luthers Sämtliche Schriften*, 15:1200–1201. 23 vols. Saint Louis: Concordia, 1899.

9) **Thomas Murner** *(1475–1537)*, a member of the Franciscan order, shared Luther's critique of moral practices in the medieval church, but he turned his gift of satire against the Wittenberg professor for the threat he posed to Murner's sense of order in church and society and his concern for proper Christian behavior. Source: Murner, Thomas. *Kleine Schriften (Prosaschriften gegen die Reformation)*. Edited by Wolfgang Pfeiffer-Belli. 1927. Reprint-Lit. Kritische Gesamtausgaben elsässischer Schriftsteller des Mittelalters und der Reformationszeit Reprint, Karben: Wald, 1997.

10) **Friedrich Myconius** *(1490–1546)* was an early convert to Luther's program for reform, pastor and superintendent in Gotha. Quotations are taken from Myconius, Friedrich. "Friderici Myconii, Historia Reformationis vom Jahr Christi 1517. bis 1542," edited by Ernst Salomon Cyprian. In *Historischer Bericht vom Anfang und ersten Fortgang der Reformation Lutheri*, part 2, by Wilhelm Ernst Tentzel. Leipzig: Gleditsch & Weidmann, 1718.

11) **Urbanus Rhegius** *(1489–1541)* left his post as pastor in Augsburg after aiding in the establishment of the Reformation in that city and became superintendent of the churches of the duchy of Braunschweig-Lüneburg in 1530. He visited Luther at the Coburg castle on his way to his new position at the court of the duke of Braunschweig-Lüneburg. Sources: Rhegius, Urbanus. *Anzeigung, daß die römische Bulle merklichen Schaden . . . gebracht habe und nicht Doktor Luthers Lehr*, Augsburg 1521, cited in Zschoch, Helmut. *Reformatorische Existenz und konfessionelle Identität. Urbanus Rhegius als evangelischer Theologe*

in den Jahren 1520 bis 1530, 39. Beiträge zur historischen Theologie 88. Tübingen: Mohr/Siebeck, 1995.

12) **Georg Spalatin** *(1484–1545)*, as advisor and confessor to Elector Frederick the Wise, formed the vital link between Luther and his prince. At Frederick's death Spalatin became pastor in Altenburg while maintaining a key role in decisions made in Wittenberg and elsewhere regarding Luther's program of reform. Source: Spalatin, Georg. "Georgii Spalatini, Annales Reformationis, Oder Jahr-Buecher von der Reformation Lutheri," edited by Ernst Salomon Cyprian. In *Historischer Bericht vom Anfang und ersten Fortgang der Reformation Lutheri*, part 2. Leipzig: Gleditsch and Weidmann, 1718.

13) **Cyriakus Spangenberg** *(1528–1604)* was the son of Johann, who introduced Luther's teaching into the imperial town of Nordhausen and ended his career in Mansfeld county as ecclesiastical superintendent. He drew Cyriakus there as pastor, first in Eisleben, then in Mansfeld, where the son preached sermons on Luther's baptismal day and death day for twelve years. These sermons were published individually and then in a collection titled *Man of God, Luther* [*Theander Lutherus*]. Others of his works contained comments on the reformer as well. Sources: Spangenberg, Cyriakus. *AdelSpiegel*. Smalcald: Schmück, 1591, 1594; Spangenberg, Cyriakus. *Theander Lutherus: Von des werthen Gottes Manne Doktor Martin Luthers Geistlicher Haushaltung vnd Ritterschafft*. Ursel: Heinrich, 1589; Spangenberg, Cyriakus. *Warhafftiger Bericht von den wolthaten / die Gott durch Martin Luther seligen/ fürnemlich Deudschland erzeigt/ vnd von der Schedlichen groben vndanckbarkeit/ fu[e]r solche grosse gaben geschrieben*. Jena: Rhebart, 1561.

Luther himself is cited from the standard scholarly edition of his works in the original languages: *D. Martin*

Introduction

Luthers Werke (Weimar: Böhlau, 1883–1993), with the use of English translations. Citations are designated by WA. Luther's Smalcald Articles and his catechisms are edited in the sixteenth-century collection of documents that defined officially the teaching of the Lutheran Church. They appear in modern edition in Dingel, Irene, ed. *Die Bekenntnisschriften der Evangelische-Lutherischen Kirche* (BSELK). Göttingen: Vandenhoeck & Ruprecht, 2014; English translation (ET): *The Book of Concord* (BC). Edited by Robert Kolb and Timothy J. Wengert. Minneapolis: Fortress, 2000.

English translations include:

Luther's Works. Edited by Jaroslav Pelikan and Helmut T. Lehmann. Saint Louis/Philadelphia: Concordia/Fortress, 1958–1986. This has twenty supplementary volumes, some already in print, others yet to appear. Citations are designated by LW.

The Annotated Luther. Edited by Hans J. Hillerbrand et al. Minneapolis: Fortress, 2009–2016. Citations are designated by *Annotated Luther*.

The Complete Sermons of Martin Luther. Edited by John Nicholas Lenker. 1905–1909. Reprint, Grand Rapids: Baker, 2000.

Sermons of Martin Luther: The House Postil. Edited by Eugene Klug. Grand Rapids: Baker, 1996.

Festival Sermons of Martin Luther: The Church Postils. Translated by Joel R. Baseley, Dearborn, MI: Mark V Publications, 2005.

Introduction

SUGGESTIONS FOR FURTHER READING

Among the countless Luther biographies, the story and significance of the Wittenberg reformer's life are best presented, in my opinion, in Scott H. Hendrix, *Martin Luther: Visionary Reformer* (New Haven: Yale University Press, 2016). I also find that Hermann J. Selderhuis's *Martin Luther: A Spiritual Biography*. Wheaton, IL: Crossway, 2017 presents his life well; as does Oberman, Heiko Augustinus, *Luther: Man between God and the Devil*. Translated by Eileen Walliser-Schwarzbart. New Haven: Yale University Press, 1989 (German, 1982). The classic rendering of the details of his career can be found in the three volumes of Martin Brecht's *Martin Luther*. Translated by James L. Schaaf. 3 vols. Philadelphia: Fortress, 1985–1993. (German ed., 1981–1987.)

Readers can also consult the following with profit:

Bainton, Roland. *Here I Stand: A Life of Martin Luther*. 1950. Reprint, Peabody, MA: Hendrickson, 2009.

Kittelson, James M. *Martin Luther: The Story of the Man and His Career*. Minneapolis: Fortress, 1986. Revised by Hans Wiersma. Minneapolis: Fortress, 2016.

Lohse, Bernhard. *Martin Luther: An Introduction to His Life and Work*. Translated by Robert C. Schultz. Philadelphia: Fortress, 1986. (German ed., 1980.)

Schwiebert, Ernest G. *Luther and His Times: The Reformation from a New Perspective*. Saint Louis: Concordia, 1950.

Luther's theology is treated as a whole in the following works:

Introduction

Althaus, Paul. *The Theology of Martin Luther*. Translated by Robert C. Schultz. Philadelphia: Fortress, 1966. (German ed., 1962.) (See also Althaus's *The Ethics of Martin Luther*. Translated by Robert C. Schultz [Philadelphia: Fortress, 1972]).

Barth, Hans-Martin. *The Theology of Martin Luther: A Critical Assessment*. Translated by Linda M. Maloney. Minneapolis: Fortress, 2013.

Bayer, Oswald. *Martin Luther's Theology: A Contemporary Interpretation*. Translated by Thomas H. Trapp. Grand Rapids, Eerdmans, 2008.

Forde, Gerhard O. *Where God Meets Man: Luther's Down to Earth Approach to the Gospel*. Minneapolis: Augsburg, 1972.

———. *Justification by Faith: A Matter of Death and Life*. 1982. Reprint, Ramsey, NJ: Sigler, 1991.

———. *Theology Is for Proclamation*. Philadelphia: Fortress, 1990.

Kolb, Robert. *Martin Luther: Confessor of the Faith*. Christian Theology in Context. Oxford: Oxford University Press, 2009.

Lohse, Bernhard. *Martin Luther's Theology: Its Historical and Systematic Development*. Translated by Roy Harrisville. Minneapolis: Fortress, 1999.

Paulson, Steven. *Luther for Armchair Theologians*. Illustrated by Ron Hill. Louisville: Westminster John Knox, 2004.

Introduction

Watson, Philip S. *Let God Be God! An Interpretation of the Theology of Martin Luther.* Fernley-Hartley Lecture 1947. Philadelphia: Muhlenberg, 1947.

For shorter essays treating individual aspects of Luther's thought, see Robert Kolb et al., eds. *The Oxford Handbook of Martin Luther's Theology.* Oxford Handbooks. Oxford: Oxford University Press, 2014; and Derek R. Nelson and Paul R. Hinlicky, eds. *The Oxford Encyclopedia of Martin Luther.* New York: Oxford University Press, 2017.

I am grateful to my colleague Jason Broge for his suggestions on how to approach this kind of work and to my research assistant Christian Einertson for his careful reading of the manuscript and many suggestions for improvements.

Chapter 1

Stations of Childhood and Youth

LATE MEDIEVAL CUSTOM AROUND the village of Möhra, nestled in the hill country at the northwest corner of the Thuringian Forest, dictated that the youngest son inherit the farm. Therefore, Hans Luder, eldest son of one of the four most well-off peasant families in the village, on his mother's side grandson of the Zieglers, perhaps the most prosperous in Möhra, left home to seek his livelihood elsewhere. He married Margarete Lindemann from Eisenach, a town a little less than ten miles north of Möhra, where his father may well have gotten to know the Lindemann family as he took his produce to market there. The Lindemanns, a merchant family, had sent at least one son on for university education at the University of Leipzig and a career as a counselor at the Saxon ducal court.

Why Hans and Margarete moved north to the county of Mansfeld, first to Eisleben, where their son Martin was born and then to the town of Mansfeld, where he grew up, is unclear. Mansfeld county was boom country at the time. New mining techniques enabled men to penetrate more deeply into the earth to find the stores of metals, copper among them, in Mansfeld. Margarete's uncle Anton

Lindemann had come to Mansfeld and established himself as a smelter-master at the end of fifteenth century. He may have aided the young couple in finding a place in the hustle and bustle of the developing industry in Mansfeld.

In any case, Hans Luder moved quickly from mining the earth to smelting copper ore. He sometimes struggled with bankers practicing the developing procedures of early modern capitalism, but he succeeded in building a business that he passed on to his younger son Jacob. His older son, Martin, he had destined for a university education in law, perhaps following consciously the model of his Lindemann relatives. He was hoping for a lawyer who could administer his growing business or win a fine post in the early modern bureaucracy of the Mansfeld counts or their Saxon ducal neighbors. Yet his business fell on hard times, and his son rose even higher in the late medieval world, to become a university professor, a professor in the queen of the sciences, theology.

Born November 10, 1483, and baptized the next day, the festival of Saint Martin, the first of Hans's and Margarete's nine (or more) children, Martin changed the spelling of his name to *Luther* in his midthirties. He was following the custom of blossoming scholars at the time by taking a Greek model for his name—transforming "Luder" into "Luther" because his theological development was liberating him from old scholastic methods through the insights of those called biblical "humanists," and he saw himself a "free man" (in Greek, *eleutherios*). Almost three decades earlier, little Martin had begun school at age seven, walking the couple hundred meters up the hill, past the doors of Saint George's Church, to the school, just across the valley from the counts' castle perched high on the opposite bluff. Castle, church, school, and the bustle of a boomtown with its peasant miners formed Martin Luther's consciousness.

Stations of Childhood and Youth

His religious upbringing in a home with typical medieval piety cultivated in him a sense that he needed to perform the sacred rites and other religious activities that would endear him to God. Divine favor could be expected in return for little Martin's proper attention to his religious duties. Bible stories shaped his thinking as he heard them told at home, in school, and in church. But he probably did not distinguish David battling Goliath sharply from the mythical tale of Saint George slaying the dragon, as the latter's story was depicted in the church up the hill. Little Martin learned that his attendance at mass and occasional confession of his sins to the priest would contribute to guaranteeing his pathway through life and purgatory into heaven.

His image of what it means to be Christian took form in the pious practices of his home and the basic religious instruction in the school. Changes in that image had certainly taken place in the seven centuries since Frankish conquerors had baptized whole villages and clans of Thuringian residents, but the structures of the faith had retained forms inherited from ancient Germanic religions. The church had lacked adequate personnel to catechize and preach in the first centuries of Thuringian Christianity. This resulted in Christian names and concepts being placed into the traditional religious configuration of human life. This worldview inherited from the earlier Germanic religious perception of reality presumed that contact with the divine was established and maintained by human beings through proper performance of sacred rituals and religious activities. Moral performance played a role as well in practicing the faith in a way that pleased God. But it was attending mass, observing appointed fast days, going on pilgrimages to sacred places near or far, and similar religious activities played the key roles in the individual's relationship to God. God's grace was more often mentioned than understood.

All Christians had access to heaven if they received absolution for mortal sins from their priest. But all anticipated extensive time in purgatory on their way to heaven. There they would receive the temporal punishment earned by their sins. The guilt of these sins had theoretically been taken away by the absolution pronounced by their priest. The shorter but steeper path toward heaven lay through the monastery or service as a priest. Those in the holy orders or in callings of priest, monk, or nun were obligated to keep the "evangelical counsels" above and beyond God's commandments. These "counsels" included strict obedience to superiors, abstinence from all sexual relationships, and poverty. Observing these counsels would accelerate the winning of the merit necessary to come before God's terrible throne of judgment. Hans Luder, like most of his contemporaries, occasionally expressed his contempt for priests, but he supported the local church. He paid his dues as a member of a fraternity in Mansfeld that funded masses for departed members to help win their release from purgatory.

The fifteenth century witnessed a growing spiritual restlessness. More and more people were striving harder and harder to do sufficient good works to merit God's grace. They hoped that their striving would bring forgiveness and the ability to perform truly good works that would please God and qualify them for heaven. But uncertainty about the true worth of their performance haunted them. Therefore, church officials were making grace easier and easier to obtain. For instance, they reduced the required performance or cash payment for "indulgences." Indulgences released those who purchased them from obligations that met God's demand for temporal punishment after sins had been forgiven by a priest in the sacrament of penance.

Stations of Childhood and Youth

Hans and Margarete Luder's son grew up with an extremely sensitive conscience that found cheaper grace no help for himself, a poor sinner in the presence of a rightfully angry and unaccepting God. Young Martin saw this God depicted on many an altarpiece as Christ with the sword of judgment in hand. Luther's world took seriously the invasion of daily life not only by the straying of the pious themselves but also by the demonic. In addition, demons took possession of people or interfered with the normal processes of nature and human activity. But his perception of his own failings and shortcomings dominated young Martin's consciousness. Life was fragile, death an imminent and horrific threat.

Little Martin learned the basics of Latin grammar and a smattering of rhetoric and logic in Mansfeld. Then he went off with his friend Hans Reinecke to attend school in Magdeburg, one of the five largest metropolises in the German empire, for a year, 1497–1498. After that year he made his way to his mother's hometown, Eisenach, to gain solid preparation for university education. His three years in Eisenach provided him a firm basis for his further education. Whether or not one of his instructors at Eisenach's Latin school, attached to the church of Saint George, actually doffed his hat out of respect for the future accomplishments of his pupils (as some sixteenth-century reports relate), Martin received his grounding in the basics of medieval learning by studying the trivium—the language arts of grammar, logic or dialectic, and rhetoric—and the quadrivium—the mathematical arts of arithmetic, geometry, astronomy, and music.

Why he did not live with his Lindemann relatives is not known. The family of Heinrich Schalbe, with whom he did board, provided him with a loving atmosphere and a stimulating spiritual environment. Heinrich Schalbe was entering into the last of his four years as the chief mayor of Eisenach; it is likely that a place in his home came only with the kind of connections that the Lindemann family could have supplied. As part of the leading circles of civic government, and fitting for their station in life, the Schalbes were absorbing the fruits of the new methods of teaching and learning generated by groups of "biblical humanists." These were scholars interested in the humanities, committed to recovering and reading original sources from the ancient world in the ancient languages: Latin, Greek, and Hebrew. They cultivated good communication, emphasizing rhetoric because they found it necessary to turn what could be logically formulated into words that persuaded and moved hearers. In Heinrich Schalbe's household his daughter Ursula and her husband Kunz von Cotta also befriended the family's young boarder. Ursula's little brother Caspar and Martin trekked together to the school of Saint George nearby each day.

The Schalbes had organized a circle of pious friends, and they turned to friars from the Franciscan cloister in the town to direct their meditation and pious exercises. Confined in the Franciscan cloister at the time was a charismatic brother, Johann Hilten, who died during Luther's time in the town. The young schoolboy may never have met Hilten, but he undoubtedly heard of his call for reform according to a strict adherence to monastic discipline. Young Martin must also have heard of Hilten's prediction that soon, as the world was about to come to its end, a prophet would arise to prepare the way for Christ's return.

Among Eisenach's churches, the foundation of Saint Mary also offered pupils a source of spiritual care. Foundation churches were established by special endowments for the saying of masses to relieve those suffering in purgatory and for other pious purposes. At Saint Mary's Church

Stations of Childhood and Youth

Father Johannes Braun organized exercises in singing and prayer for the pupils of Saint George's School. He and Luther formed a friendship that extended over more than a decade. Luther's musical talents blossomed in such a circle. So did his efforts to express his devotion to God.

In 1501, at age seventeen, typical for his time, Martin Luder from Mansfeld entered his name in the matriculation records of the University of Erfurt. At that time the university was well-established, a center of learning in the German-speaking lands. It had been founded in 1392, as the fifth "German" university after Prague (1348), Vienna (1365), Heidelberg (1386), and Cologne (1388). A municipal university in a city officially under the domination of its overlord, the archbishop of Mainz, it was not immune to the tensions within the city between merchants and artisans and between the rival ambitions of the neighboring electors of Saxony and the archbishops. Magdeburg had prepared the matriculating student for life in the big city to some extent, but grasping the finer points of municipal life seemed to elude the consciousness of this boy from a rural mining village.

His course of studies drove him more deeply into the subjects of the trivium and quadrivium so that he would be able to apply the knowledge and skills cultivated in these lectures for his training in the upper faculty of law. The university existed to develop those trained in theology, law, and medicine for service to society. Indeed, some students left the university satisfied with the training in the liberal arts, for they planned to become teachers in the growing number of town schools that provided university preparation for some and schooling in the basics for others—from the merchant and artisan families of the towns.

Martin Luder from Mansfeld concentrated on his studies. His life at the bursa or student house of Saint

George (others suggest he lived at the Amplonian College) included a strict discipline of morning and evening prayer. Luther later complained that university students had indulged in excessive drinking and illicit sex, but his reputation at the time indicates that his piety restrained him from risking more wrath from heaven than his own insufficient devotion to God was earning him. In 1502 the university awarded him the degree of bachelor of arts; three years later, the completion of his master of arts degree, as second in a group of seventeen, had deepened his command of Aristotelian philosophy in the school of the "modern way" (*via moderna*), the system shaped initially by the English philosopher and theologian William of Ockham (ca. 1288–1347).

Luther had hardly begun his study of the law before he made a dramatic shift in the direction of his life. His terror in the face of God's judgment overcame the wishes of his parents that he become a legal expert and hurled him into monastic orders.

INTERVIEWS

Doctor Luther, please introduce yourself. I am the son of a farmer; my great-grandfather, my grandfather, and my father were real farmers. Actually, I should have become a village head, a sheriff, or whatever they would have in a village, a function that would have placed me just a bit higher than others. But my father moved to Mansfeld, and he became a miner. That's where I come from.[1]

Please tell us something about your upbringing. My parents brought me up so strictly that it sometimes scared me. My mother once hit me until I bled simply because I had secretly taken a nut. Because of this hard-nosed

---

1. WA TR 5:558, Nr. 6250.

discipline, they finally drove me into the monastery. Even though they meant well, it made me scared. They did not know the appropriate relationship between someone's character and the manner in which one should be disciplined. You should punish in such a way that you place the apple beside the rod. It is bad if children and pupils in school lose their spirit because of their parents or teachers. There have been bungling schoolmasters who spoiled many excellent talents by their meanness. Ah, what a time we had on Fridays with the lupus [the "lupus" {wolf} was a pupil appointed to note who spoke in German or misbehaved, so that the worst pupil in the class was given an wooden image of a jackass to wear around his neck until he caught another pupil speaking German] and on Thursdays with the parts of Donatus [Aelius Donatus, a fourth-century author of a standard medieval Latin grammar]. Then they asked each pupil to parse precisely, according to Donatus, *legeris*, *legere*, *legitur* [standard Latin forms], and we even said *lecti mei ars* [a construction that Luther may have invented or perhaps borrowed from the contemporary poet Hans Sachs of Nuremberg]. These tests were nothing short of torture. Whatever the method that is used, it ought to take into account the difference in aptitudes and teach in such a way that all children are treated with equal love.[2]

Doctor Luther, children often have a kind of unpleasant memory of childhood; since your parents, despite sixteenth-century circumstances and the difficulties of travel, often visited you in Wittenberg and enjoyed conversing with Katharina and playing with their grandchildren, can we presume that the relationship with your father improved? It did. For example, my father's death has made me extremely sad, not only because of my father's nature but also because of his unique affectionate love and because through him,

2. WA TR 3:415–16; LW 54:235, Nr. 3566a.

my Creator has given me everything that I am and have. And even though it comforts me that he wrote that he was prepared to die in Christ in the strength of his faith, the grief and the memories of that extremely loving relationship with him have affected me intimately so much that I have hardly ever despised death as at the time of his death.[3]

Pastor Dietrich, you were with Luther at Coburg castle when he received news that his father had died. How did he react? As soon as he saw that the letter was from Hans Reinecke [his boyhood friend from Mansfeld], he said to me, 'Oh, no, my father is dead.' Immediately, he grabbed his Psalter, went to his room, and cried so hard that he suffered a headache the following day. On the Saturday before Exaudi Sunday [the Sunday before Pentecost] the administrator of the castle was with us for supper, and the Doctor related, among other things, that on the night before his father's death [a week earlier] he had dreamt that a huge tooth had fallen out, so huge that he could not have imagined it. On that Sunday his father had died.[4]

Pastor Mathesius, what impressions did you get of Luther's childhood from your time in the Black Cloister? Our merciful and bountiful God blessed the mining operation of Luther's father and gave him two smelting ovens in Mansfeld. So, Hans Luther, as a genuine mining man, raised the little son, whom he had had baptized in the fear of God, with what he had gained from his business. When the son reached the right age, the father sent him to Latin school with his own ardent prayers, where with vigor and zest the little guy learned the Ten Commandments, the Creed, and the Lord's Prayer, along with the children's grammar of Donatus, his arithmetic, and Christian singing. Even though the truth had been obscured under the Antichrist, God had

3. WA Br 5:351, Nr. 1584.
4. WA Br 5:379, 16–19, Nr. 1595.

Stations of Childhood and Youth

wondrously preserved the holy catechism in the schools along with the baptism of infants in parish churches.[5]

Doctor Luther, do you have memories of your image of God as a child? In my childhood I had gotten used to blanching and becoming frightened whenever I simply heard the name of Christ mentioned. For I had not been taught anything else other than that I had to see him as a strict and wrathful judge.[6]

Professor Melanchthon, you also enjoyed a warm relationship with Luther's parents. What is your memory of them? In his mother, Margarethe, all the other virtues of an honest woman came together: modesty, fear of God, and prayer in particular, so other upright women looked to her as an example of virtues. She answered my question about the time of her son's birth. She could remember that it was in the night of November 10 after eleven o'clock but was uncertain of the year. His brother Jacob, an upright and reliable man, said that the family believed that he was born in 1483. After he was at the age when he could learn, his parents schooled their son Martin in their home in the knowledge and fear of God and in the duties that other virtues impose. As is customary in good families, they made certain that he learned to read, and his father brought him as a rather young boy to the elementary school of Georg Aemilius. At that time, however, elementary schools in Saxon towns were of limited quality, so when Martin was fourteen years old, he was sent to Magdeburg along with his friend Johannes Reinecke.[7]

Pastor Spangenberg, you became pastor in Mansfeld after Luther's death. Did you ever reflect on what it meant that Luther grew up in a mining village? It is indeed noteworthy

5. Mathesius, *Historien*, IIb–IIIa.

6. WA 40,1:298.

7. CR 6:156–57; *Luther's Lives*, 15.

that the most outstanding worker on the mountain of the Lord before the end of the world was the son of a man who worked in the mountain mines. In Jeremiah 51 the prophet speaks of the destruction of historical Babylon and the help that the Armenians gave the Persian king in that destruction. That can symbolize the destruction of the spiritual Babylon [the papacy, in Spangenberg's view], for the prophet speaks of Ashkenaz and Minni [Jer 51:27], who plundered and devastated Babylon. Ashkenaz refers to the Germans . . . and the Miini come from Manuus, the son of Ashkenaz, from which this county of Mansfeld gets its name. That is what the miners are called who have their ovens in the village and in their smelting huts. From these German Minni or miners God brought forth Doctor Luther, who struck the great blow against the Roman Babylon that practiced the most horrible idolatry in the mass, the practice of celibacy, and other teachings of the devil and human deceitfulness [1 Tim 4:3].[8]

Doctor Luther, do you recall what schooling was like when you began to learn your ABCs? By the grace of God, it is now possible for children to enjoy and have fun when they are learning languages or other subjects in the curriculum, or history. Today the schools are not what they once were, a hell and purgatory in which we were tormented with learning cases and tenses, and yet learned less than nothing despite all the whipping, trembling, anguish, and misery. If we take so much time and trouble to teach children card-playing, singing and dancing, why do we not take as much time to teach them reading and other disciplines while they are young and have the time and are apt and eager to learn? . . . I would have children study not only languages and history but also singing and music together with all the mathematical subjects. For what is all this but play for children?

8. Spangenberg, *Theander Lutherus*, 276b–77a.

Stations of Childhood and Youth

The ancient Greeks trained their children in these subjects, and they grew up to be people of wondrous ability, fit for everything. How I regret now that I did not read more poets and historians, and that no one taught me them. Instead, I had to read at great cost, toil, and harm to myself that devil's dung, the philosophers and sophists, from which I have done all I can do to purge myself... My idea is to have the boys attend school for one or two hours during the day and spend the rest of the time working at home, learning a trade, or doing whatever is expected of them. In this way, study and work will go hand-in-hand while the boys are young and able to do both. Otherwise, they spend at least ten times as much time anyway with the peashooters, playing ball, racing, and wrestling. Likewise, a girl can surely find time enough to attend school for an hour a day and still take care of her duties at home. She spends much more time than that anyway sleeping, dancing, and playing. Only one thing is lacking, the serious desire to train the young and to benefit and serve the world with able men and women. The devil very much prefers coarse blockheads and ne'er-do-wells so that people will not get along too well on earth.[9]

At that time pupils sometimes went from house to house singing, did they not, to get support? I remember as a boy in Mansfeld when we sang in order to collect sausages. A townsman jokingly cried out, "What are you boys up to? May this or that evil overtake you!" At the same time he ran toward us with two sausages. With my companions I took to my feet and ran away from the man who was offering us this gift. This is precisely what happens to us in our relationship to God. He gave us Christ with all his gifts, and yet we flee from him and regard him as our judge.

Professor Melanchthon, did Luther tell you much about his schooling in Eisenach? In the school at Eisenach he

---

9. WA 15:47–48; LW 45:369–71.

studied for four years with an instructor who taught grammar more accurately and skillfully than other teachers. I remember that Luther praised his intelligence. He was sent to Eisenach because his mother had been born to an upright, well-established family there. He completed his study of grammar and since he was so smart, and especially fitted for good communication, he quickly surpassed his classmates and easily excelled over the other young boys in the school, both in learning vocabulary and fluency in diction and in composing prose and verse.[10]

Professor Melanchthon, did his schooling in Eisenach prepare him well for his study at the university in Erfurt? In Eisenach he had savored the sweetness of literature. He was naturally afire for learning, and he looked forward to the university as the fountain of all learning. With the power of his mind he would have been able to comprehend the whole curriculum, one subject after another, if he had found proper teachers. Perhaps the gentler nature of learning the liberal arts and studying rhetoric would have profited him by mitigating the intensity of his nature. But at Erfurt he encountered logic in a form that cultivated cantankerousness. He grasped it quickly since the wisdom of his mind mastered the rationales and foundations of its rules better than did the minds of his fellow students. But since his mind was eager to learn, he went after more and better things. He read the many works of the ancient Latin writers, Cicero, Virgil, Livy, and others. He did not read them as most boys do, picking out the words only, but he read them as instruction in the way one is to live. Because he was looking for the advice and maxims of these authors more closely, and because of his reliable and tremendous memory, he read many authors and retained what they had written in his head. Therefore, he stood out among the

---

10. CR 6:157; *Luther's Lives*, 15.

Stations of Childhood and Youth

young students, and his intelligence commanded respect throughout the university.[11]

Pastor Spangenberg, you recalled hearing the story of the Franciscan Johann Hilten, who died in confinement in Eisenach while Luther studied there? There was a pious, Christian monk in Eisenach, named Johann Hilten, who long before Luther had arrived there prophesied what an outstanding theologian he would be. For Hilten, a good and pious man, had said too much against certain abuses in the practice of the monks, and they put him in a terrible prison because of that. There he became very ill. He summoned the Father Guardian and begged that they take his weak condition into consideration and mitigate his confinement. The Guardian attacked him fiercely and scolded him sharply. He asked for pardon and said that what he had done in attacking monastic practice did not amount to much and was not worth talking about in comparison with what was coming in 1516, when a monk would really nail them and reject every aspect of monastic life completely. Then they would have to listen to him and would not be able to stand against him.[12]

Pastor Mathesius, how did Luther first get to know the Bible? As a student, he did not neglect his lessons, he liked to ask questions of his instructors, and he conversed with them with great respect. He repeated what he had heard with his comrades, and when there were no public lectures being given, he went to the university library. There one time, as he was looking at the books on the shelf, so he could get to know them, he came upon a Latin Bible, and he had never in his life seen a Bible before. With great wonder, he noticed that there were many more passages, epistle and gospel lessons, than were in the regular readings

11. CR 6:157; *Luther's Lives*, 15–16.
12. Spangenberg, *Theander Lutherus*, xx.

in church. As he was looking through the Old Testament, he came upon the story of Samuel and his mother Hannah, which he read through quickly with burning desire and joy. Because this was all new, he began from the bottom of his heart to wish that our faithful God would give him his own copy of the book.[13]

Doctor Luther, what did you think of life in the big city when you got to Erfurt? As Aristotle described political rule, it has several different forms and degrees of exercising power. First, the monarchy in which a single person is lord and rules alone, as in France, England, Bohemia, Hungary, Poland, Sweden, Denmark, and other lands. Second, the aristocracy, in which those who are the most gifted and the best, who are gifted with understanding, uprightness, and virtues, exercise governance, as in Germany and the Roman Empire, and in Venice. Third, democracy, where many of the common people rule, such as in Switzerland and Ditmarschen. Fourth, the oligarchy, in which only a few have power, such as in Erfurt.[14] . . . At Erfurt I saw some rule in this way. They were hanged and had their heads chopped off because they presumed to rule according to the book and did not realize that the devil is in the world. I am saying all this against the seditious opinions of those who go off raging and know nothing but how to improve others, as they call it, and how to find fault with them.[15] . . . Erfurt is devoid of leadership; it has feet without a head. . . . Magdeburg is very prosperous, far exceeding Erfurt, for it has the right to collect taxes from surrounding villages and charge import duties and is an imperial city [which it was not in fact]. It can make expenditures that Erfurt cannot make although it

13. Mathesius, *Historien*, IIIb–IVa.

14. WA TR 4:240, Nr. 4342.

15. WA 40,2:531; LW 12:242. Luther knew of the revolt of lower classes in Erfurt in 1509 and 1510.

Stations of Childhood and Youth

has four counties under its control. Erfurt lacks the political know-how.[16]

DISCUSSION QUESTIONS

1. What are the most important similarities and differences between Luther's family life and yours?
2. Compare Luther's basic education in the trivium and quadrivium to the education you received in school.
3. What impressions do you have of Luther's actual experience of his early education?
4. What was the role of religion in the lives of most people in the late Middle Ages?
5. What would it have been like to be Luther's primary-school teacher?
6. Given his religious background and temperament, what do you think young Luther would have found most attractive about monastic life?

FURTHER READING

1. The biographies and overviews of Luther's theology listed in the introduction.
2. Hamm, Berndt. *The Early Luther: Stages in a Reformation Reorientation*. Translated by Martin J. Lohrmann. Grand Rapids: Eerdmans, 2014.
3. Siggins, Ian D. Kingston. *Luther and His Mother*. Philadelphia: Fortress, 1981.

---

16. WA TR 4:638–39, Nrs. 6391, 6392.

Chapter 2

The Cloister and Further Studies

LUTHER NEVER DESCRIBED HOW he made the decision to forsake legal studies and enter the Augustinian Eremite cloister. We do know that he was not only plagued with a deep-seated fear of the fully justified displeasure of his Creator and Judge; he was also consumed with terror over his own mortality. No doubt his suffering an accidentally inflicted knife wound at the same time two of his brothers and three of his professors died did nothing to ease those fears. It may have been that his decision to secure his salvation by entrance into holy orders moved him to make an unusual trip to visit his parents in Mansfeld in late June 1505. But perhaps some other pressing matter tore him away from the lectures on the law that he was finding less than interesting.

Upon his return to Erfurt, on July 2, 1505, in the midst of a thunderstorm, God's wrath expressed itself in thunder and lightning near the village of Stotternheim, not much more than an hour before arrival at his dormitory in Erfurt. What must have been a long-simmering decision to

The Cloister and Further Studies

take monastic vows became solidified with an oath to Saint Anne, patron saint of miners and so a part of his childhood piety. She was thought to offer protection in storms and had received special devotion in Eisenach, where Luther had spent formative years. His decision firm, after a suitable party for friends, Luther turned himself in to the authorities at the Erfurt Augustinian cloister on July 17.

The Augustinian Eremites (Hermits) enjoyed a reputation for strict adherence to monastic discipline. That may have contributed to Luther's decision to enter this particular cloister. But the Carthusians would have made his life even harsher and therefore more meritorious. His later complaints about Carthusian dependence on works for salvation would not have put him off in 1505. The Augustinians did supply a number of instructors for the university. Thus, his study in the arts faculty may have acquainted him with their house, an older, established pivotal cloister in Erfurt. It had boasted resident theologians such as Hermann of Schildesche (ca. 1290–1357), whose work on biblical interpretation had won respect. (Though Luther never mentions him, his manuscripts must have been available in the cloister library.) Brother Martin got to know Johann Jeuser von Paltz (ca. 1445–1511), resident at this time, a famous theologian and preacher. Furthermore, the Augustinians' cloister lay only a few hundred meters from the bursa of Saint George. Luther would most likely have often encountered its black-robed residents on the streets as well as in the lecture halls of the university.

To his earthly father's great displeasure and in defiance of his wishes, Luther entered the cloister. He first underwent the usual period of screening and examination that tried to weed out those who were making a wrong decision by seeking monastic discipline. He passed the tests and settled into the life of the cloister, reciting psalms and prayers in the seven hours of prayer each day. Thus, the words of Scripture became so firmly implanted in his mind that he could not think in any other vocabulary.

The Augustinian Hermits were a mendicant order; along with the Dominicans, Franciscans, and Carmelites, they were not restricted to living behind monastic walls. Instead, those who were ordained were directed into parish life as helpers for priests who could not preach or hear confession in adequate fashion or frequency. So Luther became steeped in pastoral concerns and spiritual care. He had wanted to avoid ordination. His goal of eradicating his unworthiness for God's grace had originally propelled his hopes toward the most menial of tasks and assignments in the cloister. He used the most severe measures at hand in the monastic discipline to deprive his body and torture his sensitivities in hope of purging himself of his lusts. He strove mightily to discipline his straying thoughts and feelings that diverted him from worship of God.

His seniors and superiors, some of whom knew him as a student, were not, however, about to sacrifice the talents of this gifted young prize to his own spiritual blockheadedness. They impelled him back into studies and planned his entry into the priesthood. That took place with his ordination in a chapel of the cathedral, which served the archbishop of Mainz, to whom Erfurt belonged, on April 3, 1507.

He celebrated mass for the first time on May 2. In the middle of the liturgy of the mass the newly ordained priest's awe at handling the body and blood of Christ turned to terror. Only the stern command of the assisting minster and superior drowned out the voice of God and moved him to completion. Hans Luder did bring a delegation of colleagues from Mansfeld and sponsored a festive meal. But he was not happy with his son and the lost career in law. He could not resist venting his spleen with a remark about

The Cloister and Further Studies

God's command to obey parents. The newly consecrated priest never forgot that expression of paternal displeasure.

Ordination was but one step on the way to the goals for Luther that his superiors, particularly the Vicar-General of the German province of the Augustinian Eremites, Johann von Staupitz, were planning. Staupitz was the scion of a prominent Saxon family with close connections to the Saxon court, especially to Elector Frederick the Wise. In 1502 Frederick founded his own university. His grandfather, Frederick II, had divided his lands, and son Ernst received the electoral title while Ernst's younger brother Albert received the Saxon university in Leipzig, founded in 1409. But Frederick the Wise wanted his own university. It—particularly its faculties of law, theology, and medicine—would attract experts to his lands and provide them with locally trained leadership. The elector commissioned Staupitz to organize the faculty of theology at the infant university. It claimed the name *Leucorea*, Greek for "white mountain," which the town of "Witten-berg" claimed as the origin of its name despite its location in the flats of the Elbe river.

Staupitz had taken this assignment seriously, although his duties as Vicar-General of his order left him little time for instruction. These duties, in his own view, imposed upon him the necessity of working for reform in the church. He was dedicating much energy to finding leaders within the order to organize new cloisters and to bring the study of the apostle Paul and the namesake of the order, Augustine, to invigorate older Augustinian communities. Luther fit the bill for that program. Staupitz, wishing to escape the burden of his Wittenberg professorship, had special designs for him. Luther seemed to be a good choice as his successor, and therefore he needed a doctorate. Staupitz constructed a team that included some who became avid and active supporters of Luther's program of reform, including Wenceslaus Linck, later pastor in Nuremberg, and Johannes Lang, who led reform efforts in Erfurt.

Whether his rapid progress through the degrees of *Baccalaureus biblicus* and *Baccalaureas sententiarius* (both in 1509), necessary steps toward the doctorate, lay more on his own talent or Staupitz's impatience is impossible to determine. In 1508 Staupitz sent him to Wittenberg to teach in the arts faculty. He may have sensed beforehand that Stauptiz would place him in Wittenberg when he was fully prepared to assume lectures in front of university students, but mendicant brothers often shifted positions. He hardly could have imagined that he might spend his life in that little town.

He returned in 1509 to Erfurt, where his gifts impelled him into leadership positions and activities within the order. He assumed the office of vicar or supervisor for eleven Augustinian cloisters. He went to Rome with a brother to seek adjudication of a matter of dispute within the German province in late 1511 and early 1512, but without attaining the goals for which he was striving. Rome left a negative impression on him with its open display of a mechanical practice of church regulations and its open corruption and public sin. But this impression did not alienate Luther from the church. He continued to be a loyal son of the Holy Father in Rome and a faithful brother of the Augustinian order.

As busy as these duties made him, Luther's struggle with his own deep-seated sense of guilt and inadequacy still haunted him. The piety of the cloister was shaped by his elder Augustinian brother, Johann Jeuser von Paltz. As a preacher of indulgences, Paltz served in the German sales campaign of Raimund Peraudi, the papal legate who supervised the proffering of several indulgences in the closing decades of the fifteenth century. Peraudi and Paltz recognized the widespread crisis of pastoral care besetting the German population. They worked on devising new methods to make grace cheaper, both in terms of what individual believers were expected to do to earn grace and in terms of the amount of money charged for the papally granted certificate of indulgence, essentially a contribution to some worthy ecclesiastical cause.

Devotion to the tenderhearted Virgin Mary and other saints with local competence or with specialized help for specific ills and evils was increasing. At the same time the suffering Christ and his wounds and agony commanded ever more attention. Through the preaching of God's merciful release from sin, through prayers for the intercession of the protecting saints, and through as much obedience to church rules and laws, as much practice of virtues, and as much holy living as a person could muster, grace was placed within reach.

Nonetheless, the framework of ever cheaper grace still required human effort. Neither spiritual discomfort and discontent nor the resulting crisis in pastoral care diminished for most people. Luther found some relief through a stream of "mystical" contemplation cultivated by a school centered in the Rhine Valley. Its style of devotion was typified by the writings of Johannes Tauler (ca. 1300–1361), a Dominican friar. Tauler and others like him emphasized the grace of God that he freely gives to those who humble themselves before him. This "theology of humility" counted such self-humbling as the one human work necessary for access to God and his mercy. Brother Martin also began to devour the works of Saint Bernard, a late eleventh- and early twelfth-century Cistercian preacher. His sermons emphasized that Christ had died to win free forgiveness of sins for his people. Bernard pointed readers like Luther to refuge from guilt and shame in the wounds of their Savior. This Christ-centered piety went into the unstable mix that was congealing in Luther's thinking as a theological foundation.

In these years not only his monastic brothers and fathers but also his instructors in theology shaped the emotions and perceptions as a theology student progressing from one degree to another. His teachers followed the scholastic method that depended on Aristotle's metaphysics and ethics for its presuppositions and principles organizing biblical raw materials. Luther had fallen in love with the Bible, but his instructors directed him to the ancient church fathers and to more recent interpreters of the Christian tradition. His instructors delivered that tradition to him and his fellow students through the organization of the ideas found in the biblical writers and the early church teachers by the eleventh century theologian Peter Lombard. His *Opinions* (*Sententiae*) gathered the statements of those teachers, sometimes contradictory, in answer to specific questions. Luther found Lombard uninteresting compared to Scripture, but his professors kept him within the established program.

His instructors mixed and matched the authorities of their discipline, as all teachers do, but they depended largely on the theology harvested from the insights of William of Ockham by Gabriel Biel (ca. 1412–1495), professor in Tübingen. His doctrine reinforced Luther's childhood piety and gave it scholarly foundation. God gives grace, they taught, to those who "do what is in them"—who do their best—"on the basis of their purely natural powers." Doing one's best gained "congruent" merit—something less than truly meritorious but regarded by God as sufficient as the human being's best effort. This congruent merit produced by these naturally produced works enabled believers to fill their faith in Christ with "condign" or truly worthy merit.

In that way they could hope to appear righteous before God's throne once they had discharged their debt of temporal punishment in purgatory.

God graciously set up this system even though, according to Ockham, he was under no compulsion to do so. Ockham and Biel emphasized God's almighty power, the Creator's independence from any law apart from the law that he had invented and to which he pledged himself. God acted by his absolute power to create covenants that laid down the laws for nature and for human behavior. These covenants determine and regulate what happens in nature and what human creatures are to do. Ockham did not interpret the world and the course of history as in any way arbitrary. Once God had, by his "ordered" or "ordained" power, established the rules, they remained valid for all time. God's covenant with human creatures established the system by which Luther strove to please God and secure his place in God's presence forever.

Within this context Luther's supersensitive conscience did not cease to vex him. His superiors and brothers did their best to refocus his understanding of his relationship with God. Staupitz's own reading of Augustine had led him to emphasize God's unconditional mercy and grace toward sinners and the basis of the individual's salvation in God's own predestining choice of the individual, not in any human performance. This theology provided Staupitz the tools to comfort scrupulous brothers such as Brother Martin. The two formed an ever-deepening relationship that made Staupitz Luther's friend, teacher, and comforter.

Luther's developing theology as one on the way to becoming a "Doctor in Biblia," "teacher of the Bible," was in its earliest formative stages when, around 1509, he received a new insight into reality. He accepted the theory that Aristotle's physics could explain one level of reality with its distinction between "substance"—the ideal form or pattern of individual things—and "accidents"—the characteristics that gave any individual expression of the form its visible and tangible attributes. But he decided that this was not the ultimate foundation of reality. Relationships with God and other human creatures, as well as with the natural creation, undergird the understanding of all reality. Beneath the world of substances with their accidents lay the relationship between each individual created person or thing and the Creator. Within this relational view of reality, Luther approached his final years of academic preparation for his appointed task of university instruction in theology.

INTERVIEWS

Professor Melanchthon, how did Luther come to enter the order of the Augustinian Eremites? After he had been awarded the degree of Master of Arts at age twenty, he began to study jurisprudence on the advice of his relatives. They thought that with such a powerful mind and eloquence, he should take on a public role in the service of society. But shortly thereafter, at age twenty-one, against the judgment of his parents and relatives, he sought admission to the cloister of the Augustinian monks in Erfurt. After being accepted, he learned the doctrine of the church through very intense study. He achieved mastery of himself through the most stringent discipline. He greatly exceeded others in every exercise of readings, introspective self-examinations, fasting, and praying. I often was amazed by his natural ability to get along with little to eat and drink since he was neither small nor scrawny in stature. I saw him go four days in a row without eating and drinking, yet he remained quite strong. I often saw that on many other days he was content with just a small amount of bread and fish. This was the occasion of his beginning that way of life which he judged to be fitting for piety and learning the doctrine of God. He recounted that, and others know it as well. Often great fears suddenly overwhelmed him as he engaged in intense meditation on God's wrath or the terrifying punishments that God threatens with the result that he about lost his mind.[1]

Is that what drove him into the cloister? He felt those terrors either from early on, or most intensely, in that particular year because a companion lost his life in some sort of accident. Thus, it was not poverty that led him into this way of life in the monastic system but rather zeal to be pious. Indeed, he dedicated himself each day to learning what was customarily taught in the schools, and he read the commentaries on Peter Lombard's *Sententiae* [*Opinions of the Fathers*]. In disputations he explained to admiring hearers the labyrinths of theology inexplicable to others. But because he sought nourishment from the godly practices of that lifestyle rather than fame as a learned theologian, he studied as if it were only incidental although he easily mastered scholastic methods. At the same time, he was passionately reading the source of heavenly teaching, the writings of the prophets and apostles, in order to train his mind in God's will and to nurture his fear of God and faith. His own distress and fears moved him to devote himself all the more to this study.[2]

Doctor Luther, what do you recall about your life in the cloister? I myself was a monk for twenty years. I tortured myself with prayers, fasting, vigils, and freezing; the frost alone might have killed me. It caused me pain such as I will never inflict on myself again, even if I could. What else did I seek by doing this but God, who was supposed to take note of my strict observance of the monastic order and my

1. CR 6:157–58; *Luther's Lives*, 17.
2. CR 6:158; *Luther's Lives*, 17.

austere life! I constantly walked in a dream and lived in real idolatry. For I did not trust in Christ; I regarded Him only as a severe and terrible judge, portrayed as seated on a rainbow. Therefore, I cast about for other intercessors, Mary and various other saints, also my own works and the merits of my order. And I did all this for the sake of God, not for money or goods. Nevertheless, this was heresy and idolatry, since I did not know Christ and did not seek in and through him what I wanted.[3]

But in the cloister, you also dedicated yourself to the study of Scripture in addition to the texts of the medieval commentators, did you not? If you want to become a Christian, you must take the Word of Christ in hand, realizing that you will never be finished learning, and then with me, you will recognize that you still do not even know the ABCs. If a person were to boast, then I could certainly do that about myself because day and night I was busy studying the Bible, and yet I have remained its student. Every day I begin like someone in primary school.[4]

Doctor Luther, can you recall your feelings as you froze while celebrating your first mass? When I read the words in the liturgy of the mass for the first time, "Therefore, O merciful Father, etc., We present to you, the living, true, and eternal One," I was utterly petrified and terror-stricken by these words. I thought, how can I as a mere human being address the divine Majesty as if I was in the presence of or in discussion with a sovereign or king?[5]

Professor Melanchthon, did Luther find any relief or help for his spiritual crisis in the cloister in Erfurt? He told me that he was often encouraged by the conversations with a certain elderly brother in the Augustinian cloister in

3. WA 45:482; LW 24:23–24.
4. WA 29:583–84.
5. WA 45:482.

Erfurt. He related his anxieties to him, and he heard from this older brother much about faith. This brother led Luther to the Creed, in which it says, "I believe in the forgiveness of sins." That brother had interpreted this article of the faith in such a way that it should not be taken only in general, that is, as the demons believe that some are forgiven or that David and Peter were forgiven. Rather, it is God's command that each one of us individually believe that his very own sins are forgiven. Luther said that his interpretation was confirmed for him by a citation from Saint Bernard, and then he pointed to Bernard's sermon on the Annunciation. You should also believe what is given to you in the midst of your sinfulness, namely, the testimony that the Holy Spirit puts in your heart, saying, "forgiveness of sins is being given TO YOU." For the apostles think in this way, that a person is justified by grace through faith. Luther said not only that he was strengthened by this statement but even that Paul's entire teaching on this was impressed upon him. For Paul so often hammers home this saying, that we are justified by faith.[6]

Did this insight strike him in a flash? Little by little, as he read and compared what is said and written in the prophets and apostles and as his faith was kindled through daily preparations, he gained more illumination. Then he also began to read Augustine's writings, both his *Commentary on the Psalms* and *On the Spirit and the Letter*. That confirmed this teaching concerning faith. He found consolation there. It had caught fire in his own heart. He did not yet completely leave the commentators on Lombard's *Opinions*. He was able to recite Gabriel Biel and Pierre d'Ailly [an early fifteenth-century theologian whom Luther frequently quoted, sometimes positively, sometimes critically] by heart practically word for word. For a long time he

6. CR 6:159; *Luther's Lives*, 17.

had been reading with great diligence the works of William of Ockham. He preferred Ockham's discernment to that of Thomas Aquinas and Duns Scotus. He also carefully read Jean Gerson [another early fifteenth-century theologian whom Luther quoted often, usually positively], but he repeatedly read the works of Augustine and retained them best of all.[7]

Pastor Myconius, what were Wittenberg and the Augustinian cloister like when Luther arrived in Wittenberg? The Augustinians had just begun to build their cloister, and there was just the dormitory, where Doctor Martin continued to live. The foundations of the church had been laid, but the space had only been leveled. In the middle of the foundation stood an old chapel, built of wood, plastered with clay. It was in need of repair, with braces for support on all sides. It was about thirty feet long and twenty wide. It had a small, old, rusty balcony in which about twenty people could stand if necessary. On the south wall was a pulpit constructed out of old unfinished planks, about a yard and a half high. In short, it looked just like the stalls that the painters paint of Bethlehem, where Christ was born, or like the little church in which Johannes Hus preached in Prague. It was also called Bethlehem chapel. In this poor, miserable, wretched chapel God in these last times had his precious holy gospel and the dear child Jesus be born again, and he let Jesus be wrapped in swaddling cloths for all the world to see as a wonderful, kind, comforting, saving child, from whom we all receive salvation, payment for sin, and eternal life. It was no great church or house of God, of which there were several hundred thousand at this time, that God chose, but he chose this poor, unsightly little chapel. From

---

7. CR 6:159; *Luther's Lives*, 17.

it, the Spirit of the mouth of the Lord went out into the world and blew away the Antichrist.[8]

Pastor Mathesius, did Luther continue his interest in the Bible once he had entered the cloister? Once he had made his monastic profession and put on the habit [his black Augustinian dress], and then in 1507 became a priest and had prayed his first mass, his brothers in the cloister took the Bible from him and pressed upon him their own sophistry and scholastic teaching, which he read diligently as an obedient brother. But when he found the right times, he hid himself in the cloister's library and stuck to reading his dear Bible devotedly and faithfully.[9]

What did he tell you about his years in the Erfurt cloister? Even though he was studying and praying day and night in the cloister and was torturing and starving himself with fasting und nightly vigils, all his conduct of the mass brought him no comfort. God sent him an old brother in the cloister as confessor, who comforted him warmly and pointed him to the gracious forgiveness of sins in the Creed and taught him from Saint Bernard's sermons that he had to believe that for himself, that the merciful God and Father had won for him forgiveness of all sins through the unique sacrifice and blood of his obedient Son and he through the Holy Spirit has this proclaimed in the apostolic church through the word of absolution. This became a living and mighty comfort in the heart of our Doctor.[10]

Doctor Luther, you put your hopes for a way out of the plague upon your conscience on the institution of monasticism and became an Augustinian friar or brother. How did you come to view monasticism later? The entire monastic life amounts to nothing but tempting God. They cannot be

8. Myconius, "Historia," 24–25.
9. Mathesius, *Historien*, VIa.
10. Mathesius, *Historien*, Vb.

continent, and yet they refrain from marriage. They also abstain from certain foods although God has created these foods to be received with thanksgiving by believers, who know the truth that everything God has made is good and that nothing received with thanksgiving is to be rejected according to 1 Timothy 4:3–4.[11] ... They laughed at married people as people who give themselves over to pleasures and lusts. But the life of married people is by no means a life given over to pleasures. No, it is full of innumerable worries and troubles, sweat, and the most arduous toil. Pleasure is no more. Monks or priests, who are leading a celibate life, have ease and pleasure overflowing. As Saint Bernard rightly and wisely said, "The monks do not live a religious life; they live of a life of pleasure." They despise and disparage other ways of life in order that they may be able to live from someone else's table and get possession of mastery in this world and earthly honors. This is without a doubt the greatest and most luxurious ease, namely, to enjoy the labors of others and to haul in the wealth of the whole world.[12]

I might have thought that the discipline and solitude of the cloister would have been just the thing to help you with your spiritual struggles. It is like gnawing at your own heart. I often suffer from sharp attacks and deep sorrows. At such times I seek the company of other people, for at times conversation with the humblest servant girl has given me comfort. A person does not have control of himself when he is downcast and alone, even if he is well outfitted with a knowledge of the Scriptures. It is not for nothing that Christ gathers his church around the Word and the sacraments, around prayers and hymns, and does not want his people to be hidden in a corner. There is just no use to being a monk or a hermit. They are inventions of Satan because they exist

11. WA 42:316; LW 2:76–77.
12. WA 44:326; LW 7:34.

outside of the way God has set up and ordered life. According to the plan of creation every person is placed in a walk of life, in the family, in society, in the church. Outside this setup, no one is a person unless he has a miraculous exemption [the gift of celibacy]. Therefore, a solitary life should be avoided as much as possible.[13]

Doctor Luther, by 1517 you were developing new ideas about how education should be conducted at the university level. What was your attitude toward Aristotelian philosophy that provided the backbone of teaching at the time by 1517? We were to believe everything, always obediently listen and not even once, by way of a mild intervention, wrangle or mutter against Aristotle and Peter Lombard's *Opinions of the Fathers*. What would they not believe, those who had taken for granted everything which Aristotle, this chief of all charlatans, insinuates and imposes on others, things which are so absurd that not even an ass or a stone could remain silent about them! . . . I wanted nothing more fervently than to disclose to many the true face of that stage actor's face who had fooled the church so tremendously with the Greek mask and to show to them all his ignominy, had I only the time! I am working on short notes on Aristotle's *First Book of Physics*, with which I am determined to enact the story of Aristaeus [in Roman mythology, the son of Apollo and Cyrene, who captured Protheus, the god of the sea] against this, my Protheus. He is the subtlest seducer of gifted people, so that if Aristotle had not been flesh, I would not have hesitated to claim that he was really a devil. Part of my cross, indeed its heaviest portion, is that I had to see brothers born with the highest gifts for fine studies spending their lives and wasting their energies in such playacting. In addition, universities do not stop burning and condemning good books but produce, or rather dream up,

13. WA TR 3:593; LW 54:268, Nr. 3754.

bad ones [possibly a reference to the burning of the books of Johannes Reuchlin at the University of Cologne a year earlier].[14]

DISCUSSION QUESTIONS

1. What kind of Augustinian brother was Luther? Would you like to have been in the cloister with him?
2. What role did the depictions of life in the cloister play in constructing the picture of Luther as reformer?
3. How important was the general crisis of pastoral care and spirituality in the time of Luther's youth for his own spiritual crisis and development?
4. What was Myconius's goal when he depicted the Augustinian cloister at Luther's time in the way he did?
5. How did Luther perceive his university education and university life in general in his day?

FURTHER READING

1. The biographies and overviews of Luther's theology listed in the introduction.
2. Hamm, Berndt. *The Early Luther: Stages in a Reformation Reorientation*. Translated by Martin J. Lohrmann. Grand Rapids: Eerdmans, 2014.
3. Oberman, Heiko Augustinus. *The Harvest of Medieval Theology: Gabriel Biel and Late Medieval Nominalism*. Rev. ed. The Robert Troup Paine Prize-Treatise. Durham, NC: Labyrinth, 1983.

---

14. WA Br 1:88–89; LW 48:37–38.

Chapter 3

The Maturation of a Theologian

IN OCTOBER 1512 LUTHER completed the trajectory he had begun in proving his qualifications for the degrees of *Baccalaureus biblicus* and *Baccalaureus sententarius*, when the University of Wittenberg granted him the degree of *Doctor in Biblia*. Promotion to each degree in the medieval university resulted not from amassing credits for individual courses or writing a major paper; instead, the examination that earned degrees came in a public oral "disputation." In this disputation, the candidate defended theses, a series of brief propositions setting forth connected assertions on a specific topic. These were sometimes composed by himself or were sometimes the work of a professor. This defense gave him opportunity to display his ability to analyze logically and defend ideas that were put to the test by challenges from the professors and senior students. According to this practice, in order to earn his degree, Luther had to demonstrate his ability to argue a case on the basis of a set of theses composed by his colleague Andreas Bodenstein von Karlstadt, the dean of the theological faculty in Wittenberg at the time, who also led the questioning. Luther successfully completed the disputation. This made him eligible for the professorship for which Staupitz had groomed him.

The entire process of moving up the academic ladder had evoked some resentment in Erfurt because Staupitz's timetable for having Luther ready to assume his position in Wittenberg did not fit into the pace preferred by the Erfurt faculty. Even some who were Luther's Augustinian brothers resisted his rapid advance. Nonetheless, Luther continued to have good relationships with many of the brothers there. Others became alienated from him when he began to float his ideas for reforming the teaching of theology and the practice of pastoral care. They recognized quickly how radical his proposals were for alterations in method and content. They sensed that his focus on teaching only the Bible and not the traditions of the church would change the practice of theology—and much more.

The Bible had claimed a place in Luther's consciousness from childhood on. The "Bible of the Poor" (altarpieces and other works of art) depicted quite a few stories from the Bible. People did, not, however, always distinguish them from the portrayals of the adventures and miracles of the legends of later saints. Luther had learned the stories while at the same time cringing inwardly before depictions of God's final judgment. Those pictures fostered a profound disquiet in his mind and heart. In school he learned more of Scripture through the psalms recited in daily worship. In addition, his teachers used texts that not only drilled grammar, syntax, and usage from the most learned Latin users into students' heads but also cultivated students' knowledge of Scripture. In the monastery the daily regimen of seven hours of prayerful devotion drilled the texts of the Psalter into his mind. The *lectio divina* (godly reading) provided the only voice permitted to be heard during meals in the cloister. It consisted of the reading of the Latin Bible (the

The Maturation of a Theologian

Vulgate) and other texts, from the ancient fathers as well as from the *Legenda aurea*, the "Golden Stories to be Read," which conveyed the stories of the saints. Luther's teaching career required treating texts from Aristotle. He taught the ancient philosopher's *Ethics* as well as his works on logic and physics in Wittenberg in 1508 and 1509. He also lectured on Peter Lombard's *Opinions* and on books of the Bible.

Most scholastic professors of theology had continued their comment on Lombard as part of their offering of lecture courses once they became *Doctores in Biblia*. Luther did not. From 1513, his lectures on the Psalms, to the end of his career thirty-two years later, his offerings to students explored only biblical texts. Medieval professors had treated the Psalms more than any other book of the Scriptures. Thus, it was natural for him to take up these texts he knew so well. Professors lectured two or four hours each week. Lectures on a particular biblical book lasted as long as the professor kept talking. This initial lecture on the Psalms lasted from summer 1513 to mid-1515. Luther's treatment of the psalm texts reflected his immersion in the philosophical and theological principles of Ockham and Biel. But what he told the students made clear that relationships with God and with other human creatures formed the substratum on which reality is grounded.

Luther continued with lectures on Paul's Epistle to the Romans (November 1515—September 1516); then he took up the Epistle to the Galatians (October 1516—March 1517). He was in the midst of lectures on the Epistle to the Hebrews (April 1517—March 1518) when the distraction of public controversy resulting from his Ninety-Five Theses on indulgences broke out at the turn of 1518. Luther returned to the Psalms in 1519, but events interrupted this lecture course in March 1521.

His notes betray a shift in his thinking in the midst of lecturing on Romans. His relational view of reality led him to leave behind a system of reconciliation with the angry Judge of heaven, and his own efforts within such a system. He turned instead to Augustine's doctrine of the unconditional grace of God. From Staupitz and from renewed reading of Augustine, he learned that God "imputed"—reckoned or counted—righteous to him. His Creator did so purely out of unconditioned love, out of unexplainable mercy, for Christ's sake. With that grace he could perform righteous deeds that demonstrated to God that he was righteous while Christ's righteousness was being imputed to him through the sacraments, particularly the sacrament of penance.

At Erfurt scholastic instruction had been complemented by the influence and interest of a number of instructors in the liberal arts who were experimenting with new methods. They included some Augustinian Hermits and also one individual at the edge of university life, Conrad Mutian. All of them were cultivating the new method of learning now labeled "biblical humanism." These biblical humanists called for a purification of teaching through a return to the original texts of ancient teachers—Galen and Hippocrates in medicine, the *Corpus Justinianum* in law, and the Bible in theology—in the original languages, classical Latin, Greek, and Hebrew. They wished for lectures on Aristotle without distraction from medieval commentaries. They also deemphasized the scholastic concentration on logic and promoted an increased sensitivity to the principles of good communication treated in rhetoric.

Luther left no trace in table talks, lectures, sermons, or letters that he knew Mutian or took part in the circle around him at the university during his Erfurt years. But the methods of the biblical humanists, the cutting edge in higher learning at the time, attracted him. He mastered the principles of the ancient rhetoricians Demosthenes, Quintilian, and Cicero. He sought out the latest presentations of Greek and Hebrew texts of Scripture. He slowly began to acquire some competence in both languages. The Latin Vulgate remained the Bible implanted in his memory from childhood and monastic devotion, but he emphasized ever more the insights he gained from the original languages.

The pioneer of Hebrew studies north of the Alps, Johannes Reuchlin (1454/55–1522), was a jurist whose hobby, biblical studies, gave him a public platform for promoting the use of Hebrew. He issued a grammar and dictionary of the language of the prophets in 1506. Luther promptly acquired a copy of it as well as a used Hebrew Bible. A French monk and exegete, Jacques Lefèvre d'Étaples (Faber Stapulensis) (ca. 1450—ca. 1537), published commentaries on the Psalms and later on Paul's letters. Luther purchased them and put them to use. Lefèvre's christological interpretation influenced Luther's reading of the text of the Psalms even though he did not follow Lefèvre's view that heard Christ's voice in every psalm.

Most important, Desiderius Erasmus of Rotterdam (ca. 1467–1536), the most prominent of the biblical humanists north of the Alps in the first decades of the sixteenth century, provided Luther with two very valuable tools. First, he composed *Paraphrases* of the New Testament. They were a kind of commentary that opened up new insights into the meaning of the Greek words of the text. Second, he edited the first printed edition of the Greek New Testament (1516, second edition 1519). Luther seized the Greek text with joy and put it to immediate use. These two scholars took cognizance of each other by recognizing their common concern for the reform of the church. But both quickly came to take seriously their differences.

Erasmus soon developed a fear that Luther's program of doctrinal reform and his more aggressive way of addressing problems in the church would elicit opposition that would crush reform efforts. In addition, Erasmus found Luther's upstart suggestions for improvements in his *Paraphrases* impertinent. To make matters worse, the Dutch scholar's friend and employer, the Basel printer Johannes Froben, gathered Luther's Latin publications into a "complete works" in 1518, the first such "complete works" produced for a living author in the Gutenberg era. Erasmus's protests blocked a second edition from Froben's presses. Other printers took up the project until the Edict of Worms made it a dangerous gamble to issue a volume of that size with Luther's name.

That did not prevent the Dutch humanist from borrowing Luther's interpretations of certain passages for later editions of his *Paraphrases* in the later 1520s and 1530s. For his part, Luther soon came to realize that Erasmus's deep concern for moral and institutional reform differed from his own call for reform of public teaching, for revision of vital elements of medieval doctrines. Similarities between the two were substantial, but beneath their common concerns lay significantly different understandings of fundamental concepts, including those of God's Word and grace.

Nonetheless, Erasmus's insights into certain biblical concepts gave Luther crucial stimulus in the development of his reading of Scripture. Erasmus taught him that the Latin word *poenitentia* did not only mean "the sacrament of penance" but, more fundamentally, "repentance." Luther had learned from Johannes Tauler that "the whole life of the believer is a life of repentance." Tauler meant that a feeling of humility in the presence of God should form the orientation for all of life. Luther deepened the concept. Erasmus gave him impetus to view the Christian life from

The Maturation of a Theologian

a new angle. From Erasmus Luther learned that the sacrament of penance is primarily the reception of absolution, rather than the renunciation of sin—necessary as that also is. Therefore, Luther focused on the concept of God's promise as the reliable foundation for faith. Erasmus aided the Wittenberg professor's reinterpretation of the word "faith" (*fides*) as well. Much more than an acknowledgment of the facticity or truth of a statement, and more than a human action that the Holy Spirit ignited in believers, the Greek word for "faith," Eramsus's works showed Luther, should be understood as *fiducia*: "trust," clinging to God's promise because of his reliability and the power of God's Word.

Luther's lectures on Romans circulated in manuscript copies in the sixteenth century but disappeared from public consciousness because they were not published until scholars rediscovered the text in the twentieth century. Luther probably did not edit these lecture notes for publication. Both professor and students may have recognized fairly quickly that his views were maturing, and that these lectures contained much of the baggage he brought with him from his scholastic training. Newly discovered insights from Augustine and deeper study of the text were sorting out scholastic baggage. Luther was retaining some elements of his instructors' thinking, discarding others, transforming still others. He had more confidence in what he had said about Galatians in lectures delivered in the subsequent months. In 1519 he published a commentary extensively revised from his lecture notes on that epistle. In fact, he observed that his printed exposition was not a traditional commentary but instead a testimony or confession of faith. His skill at plumbing the texts and explaining their significance began to attract students. His reputation as an up-and-coming theologian was spreading.

This growing reputation may have been one reason that the brightest young star on the humanist horizon, Philip Melanchthon, risked coming to the little town of Wittenberg. He came there despite the fact that the town lay at the edge of the learned world in 1518. He accepted the university's offer of a professorship in the arts faculty, teaching Greek and, when necessary, Hebrew. Melanchthon's study at the Universities of Heidelberg and Tübingen had won him a European reputation as a most promising young scholar. His contact with Reuchlin, a relative of the spouse of a relative of his paternal grandmother, provided him a critical recommendation to Elector Frederick the Wise. Frederick snatched him up as a prize who would both attract students and improve instruction at his infant university. Melanchthon knew that its earliest instructors had already had given it a humanist orientation.

Luther and Melanchthon quickly recognized that the separate agendas each had been promoting held significant traits in common. Luther sought reform in the public teaching of the church; Melanchthon longed for improvement in the public teaching of the university. Luther deepened his understanding of the biblical message from Melanchthon's store of linguistic and rhetorical insights; Melanchthon found Luther's developing theological convictions a most helpful and proper interpretation of the Greek and Hebrew texts he was reading. The two became a mutually reinforcing team of intellectual and spiritual students of Scripture.

Luther had been advancing in his grasp of the meaning of critical elements of the teaching of the prophets and apostles. Luther took old packaging and wrapped new content with the old subject matter into traditional terminology. During the Romans lectures the pairing of "law" and "gospel" took on new meaning. Medieval theologians had described the "gospel" as the law of the Old Testament now delivered by Christ. It enabled clearer performance of God's requirements for human righteousness in his sight. Luther came to the conviction that "law" denoted God's plan and requirements for the leading of the God-pleasing life. "Gospel," in contrast, proclaimed God's own actions in behalf of fallen human creatures, in the incarnation, death, and resurrection of the God-man Jesus Christ.

The law not only instructed believers in the proper way to live; it also, and primarily—reflecting Luther's own experience—crushed the pretensions of sinners. The law's accusations made them aware of their failure and inability to please God with their own actions. The gospel, it slowly dawned on Luther, was not only a presentation of God's good news. Even more than that, it actually served as the Holy Spirit's tool for creating and maintaining the trust in God's promise that constitutes the new relationship of the sinner turned back into child of God. Luther and Melanchthon saw their distinction of law and gospel as a fulfillment of Christ's command in Luke 24:47 to preach repentance and the forgiveness of sins.

During the lectures on the Letters to the Galatians and the Hebrews, the meaning of the term "righteousness" slowly dawned on Luther. He had understood righteousness as God's justified demand as Creator for perfect human obedience to his law and as the human performance of that obedience. He came to his new definition of righteousness as he wrestled with key biblical texts. He found that God's true identity or righteousness expresses itself in mercy, love, and freely bestowed favor, without condition or human merit. That is who God is: mercy and love in person. He then perceived a distinction of two kinds of human righteousness. This distinction grew out of his Ockhamist understanding of God as the almighty Creator. Ockham had gone astray, Luther believed, by positing the necessity of human obedience to earn God's grace and love. Instead, righteousness comes to the sinner "from outside" (*aliena*) and is passively received (*passiva*) as a child receives identity from parents. Parents set no conditions when they bring a child to life. Righteousness in God's sight is experienced in the trust that clings to God's promise to be Father and to love the faithful. But this righteousness is twofold. Faith perceives its person as righteous in God's sight and so desires to act out this righteousness. Such actions express one's own righteousness (*activa*) that comes from one's own gratitude and obedience to God's law (*propria*).

Within the following decade Luther developed his perception that human existence transpires in two dimensions, a vertical dimension and a horizontal dimension. He labeled this distinction "two kingdoms" (*zwei Reiche*). The term is sometimes confusing because he also talked about the conflict of God and Satan in terms of two kingdoms. For this reason, it is helpful to speak of this distinction of the dimensions of human life as "two realms." The two realms of human life do not equate to these two kingdoms. God and Satan war against each other in both realms. Passively, believers receive new life and their identity as God's children in the vertical realm. They recognize who they are as God's children in making decisions in the horizontal and vertical realms as they obey God's commands to praise him and to serve and love others. Actively, in the vertical realm they worship and pray to God, and in the horizontal they care for and love God's other creatures. Law informs them of God's will and does its crushing work in both realms. Gospel bestows identity in both, as well, and moves believers to live a life of devotion to God and to care for the neighbor.

These frameworks for interpreting Scripture were integrated with what Luther called his "theology of the cross." As he first proposed his understanding of the term in 1518, it referred to God's revelation of himself in the "foolishness" and "impotence" of the cross of Christ and its message of salvation (1 Cor 1 and 2). This view of the Creator functioned alongside the parallel definition of faith, rather than reason, as the constituting factor of human personhood and personality. Aristotle's *animal rationalis* [rational living being] had become the person defined by trust in Christ. The focus on Christ's cross (and resurrection) became Luther's central explanation of Christ's atonement for sin and his restoration of sinners to faith in God. The cross also described God's use of suffering to defeat Satan in the life of the church and the lives of individual believers. Luther also referred to the cross that believers experience in their service to others.

Amid these theological developments, Luther's pastoral concern for those who were purchasing indulgences to gain release from purgatory for themselves or relatives and friends diverted his attention a bit.

INTERVIEWS

Professor Melanchthon, how and why did Luther begin his teaching career in Wittenberg? Johannes von Staupitz had helped the University of Wittenberg get started, and he was eager to promote the study of theology in the new university. He was certain that Luther excelled in intellectual acumen and scholarship, so he brought him to Wittenberg in 1508. Luther was age twenty-six. In the daily activities and lectures of the school, his intellectual acumen began to shine through even more. His judicious colleagues, for instance Doctor Martin Mellerstadt, were listening carefully to him. Mellerstadt often said that Luther's intellectual acumen was so formidable that he clearly foresaw that Luther would change the predominant form of studies [the scholastic method], which was the only method being taught in the schools at the time. In Wittenberg he first commented on Aristotle's *Dialectics* and *Physics* while not losing his dedication to reading theological works.[1]

Pastor Mathesius, did you hear stories about Luther's first impressions on his Wittenberg colleagues? Doctor Mellerstadt, who was regarded as the *lux mundi* [light of the world] and a teacher in medicine, law, and monastic sophistry, could not forget this monk's arguments and explanations at table. He often said, "This monk will show the errors of all the teachers and bring forth a new teaching and reform the entire Roman church. For he interprets the writings of the prophets and apostles and stands on the word of Jesus Christ, which no one can overturn or oppose with sophistry, Scotism, Albertinism [teaching of the thirteenth-century theologian Albert the Great], Thomism and the entire Tartaret. [Pierre Tartaret died 1522, a Parisian commentator on Thomas Aquinas, Duns Scotus, and other scholastic authors.]"[2]

Doctor Luther, how do you remember coming to the heart of your new insights into the biblical message? Although I was living an irreproachable life as a monk, I felt that I was a sinner before God and had an extremely distressed conscience. I could not have confidence that it could find peace through my performance of satisfactions. I did not love—I hated!—the righteous God who punishes sinners. Secretly, I expressed my anger with God, if not in the form of blasphemy, at least with intense grumbling. I said, "As if, indeed, it is not enough that miserable sinners, who are eternally ruined through original sin, are crushed by every kind of calamity by the law of the Decalogue, without having God add affliction to our affliction by the gospel and

1. CR 6:160; *Luther's Lives*, 17.
2. Mathesius, *Historien*, VIa.

The Maturation of a Theologian

also by the gospel threatening us with his righteousness and wrath!" I raged with a savage conscience that was in turmoil. Nevertheless, I impertinently hammered on Paul over this passage, passionately wanting to know what Paul was after. At last, by the mercy of God, as I was meditating day and night on what was holding this passage together—"the righteousness of God is revealed in it, as it is written: the righteous lives by faith" [Rom 1:17]—there I began to understand that the righteousness of God is that by which the righteous person lives by the gift of God, namely by faith. And this is the meaning: the righteousness of God is revealed by the gospel, namely, the passive righteousness with which the merciful God justifies us through faith, just as it is written: the righteous lives by faith. At this point I felt that I had been completely born again and had entered paradise itself through wide open doors. There a completely different face of the entire Scripture appeared to me. At that, I ran through the Scriptures as I had them in my memory, and I gathered together in other words parallel expressions, such as "work of God," that is what God effects in us; "power of God," by which he makes us powerful; "wisdom of God," by which he makes us wise; "strength of God," "salvation of God," "glory of God." Then, just as much as I had hated the word "righteousness of God," I now loved it and praised it as the sweetest of all words. This passage of Paul became truly the gate of paradise. Afterward, I read Augustine's *De spiritu et littera*. There, contrary to what I had expected, I found that he, too, interpreted the righteousness of God in a similar way, as the righteousness with which God clothes us when he justifies us. Although he expressed these things imperfectly and did not explain everything having to do with imputation clearly, it was nevertheless reassuring that this idea—that God's righteousness is that by which we become righteous—had been taught earlier. More fully armed by these thoughts, I began to interpret the Psalter a second time, and the work would have grown into a large commentary if I had not again been compelled to leave the task I had begun because Charles V convened the diet at Worms in the following year.[3]

Did you have one special moment when that all became clear to you? I did not learn my theology all at once. I had to ponder over it ever more deeply, and my spiritual trials were of help to me in this, for a person does not learn anything without being actively engaged with it. This is what the super-pious fail to see. They do not confront the right adversary, the devil. He would teach them well. None of the subjects in the curriculum can be learned without practice. What kind of physician would that be who stayed in school all the time. When he finally puts his medicine to use and deals more and more with the physical body, he will come to see that he has not as yet mastered the art of curing. Why should this not be the case with the Holy Scriptures, too, where God has provided a different opponent? It is therefore the greatest gift that God gives to have a text and to be able to say, "This is right. I know it." People think that they can know everything simply by listening to a sermon . . . I know that I have yet to grasp fully the Lord's Prayer. No one can master it without practicing it. The peasants put it well: "Armor is fine for a person who knows how to use it." To be sure, the Holy Scriptures are sufficient in themselves, but God grant that I find the right text for the situation I am facing. For when Satan disputes with me regarding whether God regards me with his grace, I do not dare to quote the passage, "He who loves God will inherit the kingdom of God," because Satan will at once object, "But have you really loved God!" Nor can I retort that I am a diligent reader of Scripture and a preacher. That shoe does not fit that foot.

3. WA 54:186; LW 34:337; *Annotated Luther*, 4:501–2.

I should say instead that Jesus Christ died for me and cite the Creed concerning the forgiveness of sin. That will do it![4]

Doctor Luther, you frequently praised Saint Augustine for his insights into God's grace and claimed that he pointed you to the complete dependence of human beings on the favor of God. Did you largely just adopt Augustine's understanding of the biblical message? It was Augustine's view that the law, fulfilled by the powers of reason, does not bestow righteousness, even as the works of the moral law do not make the pagans righteous, but that if the Holy Spirit lends his aid, the works of the law do make a person righteous. The question is not whether the law or the works of reason make us righteous, but whether the law, when kept with the Holy Spirit's help, justifies. I reply by saying no! Even if in the power of the Holy Spirit a person were to keep the law completely, he ought nevertheless to pray for divine mercy, for God has ordained that human beings should be saved not by the law but by Christ. Works never give us a peaceful heart. Christ would never have been sad in spirit unless he had been pressed hard by the law, to which he subjected himself for our sake.[5]

The forgiveness of sins is an ever-present theme in your teaching and preaching, is it not? In our teaching of the forgiveness of sins we have the knowledge of Christ. That is the only thing that comforts us and lift us up. Apart from the forgiveness of sins I cannot bear my bad conscience at all. The devil hounds me about a single sin until the world becomes too small for me. Afterward, I feel like spitting on myself for having been fearful over such a small thing. So only knowing Christ keeps me safe. From this I conclude: the devil and God are enemies. While God loves life, the devil hates life. Knowing God can therefore be depicted in

4. WA TR 1:147, Nr. 352.

5. WA TR 1:32; LW 54:10, Nr. 85.

such a way as if it is God's intention to be angry with me, and a person may be led to think that our Lord God and the devil are both intent on strangling us. To this, a person must reply, "Life is God's aim, and so he will not slay you. This is what knowing Christ means: by his death he has won the victory over death," and go on like that.[6]

Brother Murner, how do you regard the heart of Luther's teaching? He teaches that every person has a twofold nature, spirit and flesh, and in his soul he is called a spiritually new person, but according to his flesh and blood he is flesh, the old, outward person. He says that in Scripture the two are battling with each other, for the inner person is free and a lord over all things and subject to no one, and neither works nor wisdom make him an upright person in this life. Only faith does that. The outer person is a submissive servant in all things and subject to everyone. Here we want to answer for all those who are vexed by this way of speaking. If faith is everything and alone is sufficient to make a person a good Christian, why are good works commanded? We could then just be happy, and we would do nothing. No, dear fellow, it is not so. That would be as if you were only an inner person and completely spiritual, and that does not happen till the Last Day.[7]

Georg Benedict came from Lüneburg to study in Wittenberg at this time. Mr. Benedict, what was Professor Luther like in the lecture hall? He was a man of middle stature, with a voice which was both sharp and soft: it was soft in tone, sharp in enunciation of syllables, words, and sentences. He spoke neither too quickly nor too slowly but at an even pace, without pauses, and very clearly. He put his ideas in such proper order that each part flowed naturally out of what went before. He did not expound each part with long

6. WA TR 1:32; LW 54:10, Nr. 85.
7. Murner, *Kleine Schriften*, xx.

and tangled sentences, but he treated the individual words first, then sentences, so that a person could see how the context of the exposition arose and flowed out of the text itself. It all hung together in order—word, subject matter, natural and moral philosophy—as Philip [Melanchthon]'s dialectic teaches. For this was how he took it from a book of basic concepts, which he had prepared himself, so that he had his lecture material always ready at hand—conclusions, digressions, or moral philosophy, and also antitheses. Thus, his lectures never contained anything that was not pithy and relevant. And to say something about the spirit of the man: if even the fiercest enemies of the gospel had been among his hearers, they would have confessed from the force of what they heard that they had witnessed not a man but a spirit, for he could teach such amazing things not from himself but only from the influence of some good or evil spirit.[8]

Professor Melanchthon, you came to Wittenberg after Luther had firmly established himself as a tone setter for the theological faculty and the university. What kind of a reputation had he been building in the 1510s? When you think about that, just remember that he was thirty years old when the rank of doctor was conferred on him, recognizing a certain maturity of judgment. He himself used to tell that Staupitz commanded him to study when he was trying to escape and refused to let himself be awarded this degree. Staupitz jokingly said that God had a lot of work to do in the church and would be able to use Luther's help. This statement, even if it was said jokingly, nevertheless was true, and it presaged many changes. Then he began to lecture on the Epistle to the Romans and later on the Psalms. He elucidated these books so that, as light after a long, dark

---

8. From a manuscript discovered in 1932, recorded in Boehmer, *Der junge Luther*, 366–67.

night, so new teaching seemed to appear in the opinion of all pious and prudent people. At one point, he highlighted the essential concern of the law and of the gospel. At another point, he refuted the error that predominated in the schools and in disputations, that people merit forgiveness of sins by their own works and that they attain righteousness in God's sight by keeping the law, agreeing with the teaching of the Pharisees. Thus, Luther called the thinking of the people back to the Son of God. Like John the Baptist, he demonstrated that the Lamb of God, who takes away our sins [John 1:29], freely forgives sins on account of the Son of God, and that therefore this favor must be accepted by faith. He also explained other parts of the doctrine of the church. These beginnings of the monumental events of the time gave him great authority, especially since the teacher's character was one with what he was teaching. What he said seemed to be born in his heart, not on his lips. Admiration for his way of living elicited great changes in the thinking of those who heard him, so that as even the ancient philosophers said, "his character was, almost, so to speak, the strongest proof." Therefore, when, later on, he was altering certain traditional rites, honorable people who knew him were less vehemently opposed, and, in those statements in which they saw, with great sadness, the world torn apart, they supported him because of his authority, which he had gained by teaching well and living a holy life.[9]

Doctor Luther, it is said that your first impression of Philip Melanchthon was somewhat negative, based on his little lisp and his scrawny appearance, but that it changed quickly. What changed your mind? Four days after he arrived, he delivered an extremely learned and absolutely faultless inaugural lecture. Everyone respected and admired him greatly . . . We very quickly turned our minds and eyes

9. CR 6:160–61, *Luther's Lives*, 18.

from his appearance and person to the man himself. We congratulated ourselves on having this man, and we marveled at what he has in him . . . I certainly do not want to have a different Greek instructor as long as he is alive. I only fear that perhaps his constitution is not sturdy enough for the rough way of life in our region. I am also afraid that he has been hired for far too scanty a salary.[10]

How would you compare yourself and Melanchthon after a decade of working together? I was born to fight with the scalawags and devils. They are my assignment. Because of this, my books are so vehement and feisty. I am assigned to root out the roots and chop down the trunks of the trees, to chop away at the thorns and thickets, to fill the holes. I am the one who has to cut down the big trees, clear the path, and bring things in order. But Master Philip comes in, cool, calm, and collected. He cultivates the ground and plants; he sows and waters with enthusiasm, according to the gifts God has so richly bestowed upon him.[11]

DISCUSSION QUESTIONS

1. Would you prefer to graduate on the basis of course grades and accumulated credits or to earn your degree with your performance at a disputation like the one Luther had when seeking his doctorate?

2. What is the significance and impact of Luther's early use of the works of the "biblical humanists"?

3. Why did Luther's early relationship with Erasmus have negative aspects as well as positive aspects?

---

10. WA Br 1:192; LW 48:78, Nr. 88.
11. WA 30,2:68–69.

4. What was the issue underlying Luther's understanding of faith in Christ as at once the only way to salvation and the source of truly good works?

5. Why did Luther and Melanchthon make a good team?

6. If you see "righteousness" as related to your sense of identity or integrity as a whole human being, how important is Luther's besetting question of becoming righteous for people today?

7. Do you worry about justifying yourself to friends or others?

FURTHER READING

1. The biographies and overviews of Luther's theology listed in the introduction.

2. Spitz, Lewis W., Jr. *The Religious Renaissance of the German Humanists*. Cambridge: Harvard University Press, 1963.

3. McGrath, Alistair. *Luther's Theology of the Cross: Martin Luther's Theological Breakthrough*. 2nd ed. Oxford: Blackwell, 2011.

4. Forde, Gerhard O. *On Being a Theologian of the Cross: Reflections on Luther's Heidelberg Disputation, 1518*. Grand Rapids: Eerdmans, 1997.

5. Hamm, Berndt. *The Early Luther*. Translated by Martin J. Lohrmann. Grand Rapids: Eerdmans, 2014.

6. Kolb, Robert, and Charles P. Arand. *The Genius of Luther's Theology: A Wittenberg Way of Thinking for the Contemporary Church*. Grand Rapids: Baker Academic, 2008.

Chapter 4

The Media Revolution and the Thickets of Controversy

JOHANNES VON STAUPITZ HAD cultivated in Luther a sense of urgency for reform. That matched Luther's own mindset as he struggled with his own conscience and with the biblical text. In September 1516 his student and colleague on the arts faculty Bernard Bernhardi proposed theses for disputation that expressed central ideas he had gained from hearing Luther's lectures on Romans. These theses focused on the bondage of the human will, on its total incapacity for turning itself to God. That struck at the heart of Gabriel Biel's teaching that those who were worthy of salvation had to begin the construction of a saving relationship with God by doing the best they could by their own natural powers. Luther's conviction affirmed Augustine's insistence on total human dependence on God's grace and the Holy Spirit's power.

Bernhardi's propositions caused ripples of protest through the Wittenberg scholarly community. But in the ensuing months Luther's colleague Andreas Bodenstein von Karlstadt moved from fierce criticism to devoted enthusiasm for Augustine's writings against the "Pelagian" position of his day. It credited human beings with the ability to contribute to their own salvation. Karlstadt even began to lecture on Augustine. Another colleague, Nikolaus von Amsdorf, also turned from suspicion to warm support and spent the rest of his forty-nine years promoting his understanding of Luther's way of thinking.

A year later, in September 1517, Luther prepared theses for his student Franz Günther to defend in his promotion to the degree of *Baccalaureus biblicus*. This time the theses focused not on the content of his call for reform but on theological method. The theses decisively rejected dependence on Aristotle and imposition of Aristotelian presuppositions on biblical material. Luther did not object to many elements of the Aristotelian system. He continued to use his logic, poetics, and physics, among others of the philosopher's writings, in his teaching. But the ancient philosopher's metaphysics and ethics defined the human creature fundamentally as an *animal rationalis*, a rational being. As this rational being, a person was to find peace through conformity to the eternal law that gave stability to the universe. Luther found the absence of the person of the speaking Creator and the lack of a personal relationship with that Creator fatal to any true understanding of reality. Aristotle could serve human beings in many ways with his principles for good communication and clear thinking in the earthly realm, but he could not provide keys or clues to the heart of reality and the underpinnings of the human creature's relationship to the Creator.

It remains a mystery how Luther might have continued with this trajectory for reform because another concern pushed him into a public dispute that became far more serious, with far greater impact, than theses for students at

Wittenberg. In the summer of 1517 a preaching campaign to sell a new papal indulgence that promised full remission of punishment for sin began in central and northern Germany. Archbishop Albrecht of Mainz, younger brother of Elector Joachim of Brandenburg, a rival of Frederick the Wise, had received three ecclesiastical offices in a manner that required payment for dispensations. Albrecht had extended the power of his Hohenzollern family in competition with the Saxon Wettin family of Frederick by assuming these positions that had previously been held by two brothers of Frederick, both of whom died young. As archbishop of Mainz Albrecht automatically became chancellor of the German Empire and thus one of the most powerful people in all the German lands.

However, Archbishop Albrecht had attained this status and power outside the legal bounds set by the church (although within the bounds of the practice of the day). He had not reached the proper age to receive such appointments, and he was a pluralist, holding more than one such office at once. In addition, he had to find the money to pay the usual fees associated with assuming high clerical office. Pope Leo X needed funding for his project of building the basilica of Saint Peter in Rome. The solution for both of them came with Leo's commissioning Albrecht to market indulgences in the German Empire. Proceeds were to be divided between Leo's building project and Albrecht's payment of what he owed the papal treasury. Albrecht needed that income to supplement what he could reasonably expect in taxes and fees from his jurisdictions as administrator of the bishopric of Halberstadt, archbishop of Magdeburg, and archbishop of Mainz.

Albrecht turned to a seasoned, accomplished preacher of indulgences, the Dominican brother Johannes Tetzel. Over the course of his career, Tetzel had served as a preacher of indulgences and as inquisitor for Poland and Saxony. He had enjoyed some success, though he had once come perilously close to execution. Coincidentally, it was Frederick the Wise himself who had obtained a pardon for Tetzel when the Dominican was slated for execution on charges of adultery.

The conditions of Albrecht's instructions for the indulgence sale made the offer quite attractive. Not only release from time in purgatory, as was customary, but also forgiveness of the guilt of all sins, even that of raping the Virgin Mary, could be obtained through the purchase of the indulgence. Frederick the Wise forbade Tetzel from entering his territories. But Wittenberg citizens journeyed the thirty miles to Jüterbog in Brandenburg and returned to inform Luther, who as an Augustinian assisted the local priest in Wittenberg in hearing confession, that Tetzel had informed them that they no longer needed his absolution. His pastoral concern for his people, who were disdaining repentance and faith, impelled him to raise questions about Tetzel's, Albrecht's, Pope Leo's indulgence.

Neither the doctrinal explanation of indulgences nor regulations for the related practice was well developed at this time. Luther provoked the first longer treatise on the subject from the Dominican advisor at the papal court, Thomas da Vio, Cardinal Cajetan, whom Pope Leo sent to Germany to arrest the errant Augustinian in 1518. In October 1517 Luther proposed theses for debate, this time not for a student to defend, but for colleagues to treat in a formal disputation. Professors often used the genre of disputation to test their ideas without involving students in the need to defend them. Despite questions raised about the procedure by modern scholars, in all likelihood a university official affixed Luther's theses to the Leucorea's public bulletin boards, one of which was indeed the door of the Castle church, where university lectures and disputations took place. It was also where Frederick the Wise displayed once a year his own collection of relics. It had grown to 17,443 pieces by 1518, the veneration of which earned hundreds of annual visitors to Wittenberg over fifty thousand years of release from purgatorial pain. Frederick's display occurred on All Saints' Day; Luther's apparent choice of the eve of the festival, October 31, highlighted the urgency of his pastoral worry about the state of parishioners' relationship with God. The disputation Luther desired never took place.

The disputation genre did not require the author to set forth his convictions on the subject; its purpose was to elicit debate. Even so, Luther's Ninety-Five Theses on indulgences probably did express his deeply felt unrest over the abuse of God's Word embodied in Tetzel's indulgence offer. Such theses were normally printed in minimal quantity for local participants. Luther actually took some copies and mailed them to his own bishop, Hieronymus Scultetus of Brandenburg, and to Archbishop Albrecht, as well as to a few friends in Erfurt and elsewhere. But anonymous printers, probably in Nuremberg, Basel, and perhaps Leipzig or Augsburg, received copies from someone, almost certainly not Luther. These printers sensed a modest market for this usually unmarketable genre. No one had ever tried to distribute academic theses for a university disputation on a wider scale before. Their gamble paid off. Rapidly, Luther's pastoral concern became the talk of widespread circles of intellectuals and of common people. A media revolution was in the making as the theologian and pastor Martin Luther and the inventor and printer Johannes Gutenberg, separated by more than half a century in age—and in 1517 by the grave itself—came together as an unlikely team. Nothing in human history compared to this venture into public relations, or publicity for a person and his ideas.

It might have ended there if Luther had not perceived the potential of the printing press. Earlier he had tried publishing his lectures for his students to use, and that had served his local pedagogical purposes. He had also tried his hand at cultivating popular devotion, first with the publication of a devotional work from the school of Johannes Tauler, a fourteenth-century Dominican devotional writer. Luther titled the work *German Theology* in 1516. The next year he offered the reading public meditations on the seven penitential psalms. Neither had revealed the potential for reaching a broader public that became clear in the weeks after the printing of the Ninety-Five Theses. Luther composed a German version of his concerns about the pastoral and spiritual impact of the Tetzel indulgence, his *Treatise (Sermo) on Indulgence and Grace*, which was issued in early 1518. A Latin defense of his positions in the Ninety-Five Theses as well as other early treatises and an explanation of his concerns for the teaching and practice of the church, his *Defense of All Articles*, appeared in Latin in late 1520 and in German in early 1521. Luther slowly began to grasp the possibility of attracting widespread support for his call for reform. Printers quickly became key members of the reforming team. Luther learned to cooperate closely with them and with the local court painter, Lukas Cranach, whose woodcuts attracted readers to many of his publication.

The criticism of the indulgence attracted relatively little response. But ecclesiastical officials read these theses as an implicit challenge to papal authority. For medieval Christians, the stability of the public peace and the order of both spiritual and temporal realms hung on God's exercise of control over his church through Peter's successor, the bishop of Rome, the pope. Italian officials at the papal court led the response that soon drew German opponents into the conflict. They responded to this threat to the structure of their world with a fury and determination born of genuine trepidation over the destructive potential of any challenge to papal power and authority. Monastic humility restrained Luther's defense of himself more than it would later as German challenges became stronger.

In fact, one German challenger leaped to the defense of his personal friend, Johannes Tetzel: Konrad Wimpina, a Dominican professor of theology at the university of Frederick the Wise's rival, Joachim of Brandenburg. Rivalries between universities, in this case both recently founded, and between mendicant orders, contributed to Wimpina's eagerness to enter the lists against Luther. His disputation in defense of Tetzel's preaching and practice moved his fellow Dominicans in the Saxon province to petition Rome for Luther's excommunication. Other German theologians joined the chorus of criticism.

One of the brightest and best among them, Johannes Eck, of the rival University of Ingolstadt, had initially welcomed Luther as a fellow humanist reformer. But by late 1517 he found Luther's developing theology seriously at odds with his own defense of freedom of the will. Opposition to Luther provided a worthy means of diversion from the criticism Eck was receiving for his defense of lending money at interest, in defiance of centuries of Christian practice. As a close associate of the Fugger banking family of Augsburg, leading contributors to the spread of capitalistic practice of the day, Eck was under fire from fellow theologians. Despite Eck and other formidable foes quickly coming to the defense of the old order with sharp criticism of Luther, the Wittenberg professor's theses and their implicit call for reform won the sympathy of many. Chief among them were biblical humanists, who had been supporting criticism by Erasmus and others of many pious practices.

The papal curia in Rome instructed Augustinian officials in Rome to deal with Luther; they passed the assignment on to Staupitz. He used the regular meeting of the brothers in his province scheduled for Heidelberg in April 1518 to give Luther a sounding board. A brother from the Wittenberg cloister, Leonhard Beier, accompanied Luther to Heidelberg. Beier presented his forty theses that informed his brothers of Luther's program. Luther's theses did not touch on the issue of indulgences, and he ignored the burning issue of papal authority, which remained somewhat secondary to his pastoral concerns at this point. Instead, Beier set forth the framework of Luther's entire approach to theology, moving beyond the theses of Bernhardi and Günther that had paved the way for a summary statement of content and method. These "Heidelberg theses" spelled out Luther's "theology of the cross" (see chapter 3). His proposals about God Hidden and God Revealed and the superiority of trust in God's Word over human reason electrified the hearers, which included more than the Augustinian fellowship. Students and professors from the university and others felt compelled to explore what had become the hottest topic in Germany, what this Luther was up to. His theses won over the minds and hearts of many.

In subsequent months his critics kept up a steady stream of attacks on his person and his teaching. Luther replied with devotional literature and theological responses as well as with direct answers to their criticism. This criticism focused on Luther's growing antipathy toward a pope whom he had expected to exercise his office by endorsing faithful biblical teaching. Leo and his minions severely disappointed the Doctor in Bible from Wittenberg.

The Media Revolution and the Thickets of Controversy

In autumn 1518 Leo sent Cardinal Cajetan to the imperial diet in Augsburg to summon Luther to Rome. Frederick the Wise foiled the attempt to whisk him away to what most likely would have been lifetime confinement or death at the stake. Luther did have the opportunity to converse over several days with the cardinal. Cajetan refused serious theological discussion. He returned again and again to insistence that he had come to Augsburg to obtain a recantation or to place Luther in his custody and return him to Rome for trial. Finally, their conversation came to an abrupt end. Staupitz absolved Luther of his vows as an Augustinian brother and counseled flight. Luther fled in the dark of night.

Johannes Eck then challenged Luther and his Wittenberg colleagues to a public disputation. Luther's later archenemy, Duke Georg of Saxony, cousin and rival of Frederick the Wise, believed that ideas should not be suppressed once they had gained public attention. He invited a delegation from Wittenberg to his university in Leipzig to confront Eck in June and July 1519. Although Eck coveted the opportunity to take on Luther, his challenge to the Wittenberg faculty had officially focused on Karlstadt, its senior member. Eck easily outdebated Karlstadt on several topics before obtaining the safe conduct that permitted Luther to speak publicly. Duke Georg issued the safe conduct, and Eck had little trouble in maneuvering Luther into admitting that his challenge to papal authority and his understanding of the fallible nature of both popes and church councils resembled the teaching of the Bohemian heretic Jan Hus (ca. 1370–1415). In 1415 the Council of Constance had condemned Hus's teaching on giving the laity the blood of Christ in the mass and Hus's rejection of papal authority. Some of Hus's followers had organized militarily, and memories of their invasion of Saxony made Hus persona non grata in Leipzig for more than religious reasons. Luther returned to Wittenberg, studied Hus's writings, and found that, despite differences on some issues, including justification of sinners through faith in Christ, they shared similar views of the church.

Eck proceeded to seek Luther's excommunication in Rome. Luther proceeded to put the printing press to best advantage. Between June 1520 and January 1522 he composed six treatises that summarized the heart of his call for reform. His *On Good Works* (June 1520) contained his insistence on the performance of good works but also condemned the misimpression that they earned merit and contributed to salvation; they were products of the trust that grasped Christ's gift of righteousness, the identity as God's child. In an *Open Letter to the German Nobility* (August 1520) Luther repeated many grievances voiced earlier against papal practices and taxes, setting forth a plan for the abolition of superstitious practices inherent in the medieval piety that was centered on conformity to ecclesiastical regulations not based in Scripture. His *On the Babylonian Captivity of the Church* (October 1520) deconstructed the medieval sacramental system that was popularly perceived as delivering grace and spiritual security through the mere outward performance of sacred rituals, regardless of whether faith in Christ was present. In this way Luther was freeing believers from dependence on the hierarchical mediation of the local priest, the regional bishop, and the pope in Rome. As papal diplomat, Karl von Miltitz had been sent to Germany to enlist Frederick's support for dispatching Luther to Rome. He quickly recognized that the professor's widespread popularity would make that difficult if not impossible. Therefore, von Miltitz urged Luther to compose an appeal for reconciliation to Pope Leo. The appeal failed, but the accompanying treatise, *On the Freedom of a Christian*

(November 1520), expressed the reformer's understanding of the bestowal of righteousness and freedom from sin, death, Satan, and God's wrath that liberates believers to be bound to their neighbors in love and service.

Luther countered the rejection of his teaching on the gift of righteousness through forgiveness of sins for the sake of Christ that a theologian at the University of Leuven, Jacob Masson (Latomus), composed in 1521. His *Contra Latomus* appeared in the summer of 1521. This work explained the foundation of Luther's teaching on justification by grace through faith in Christ. Finally, his *Judgment on Monastic Vows* (January 1522) applied his concept that God calls everyone to service to others and condemned reliance on monasticism as a superior route to heaven.

While Luther was portraying his interpretation of Scripture and its implications for the church's practice in these and other publications, Eck was busy campaigning in Rome for his excommunication. Success greeted his efforts. They culminated in the papal bull *Exsurge Domine* (June 1520), which threatened formal condemnation of Eck's Wittenberg foe. The condemnation subsequently came in *Decet pontificum Romanum* (January 1521). Eck returned to German lands to publicize that success.

INTERVIEWS

Pastor Myconius, you knew Johannes Tetzel before the 1517 indulgence sale? Already in 1512, the Dominican Johannes Tetzel, the most important advertiser, manager, and indulgence preacher in Germany, was producing unbelievable amounts of money through his preaching, and it was all sent to Rome. He was preaching especially in the mining center Saint Annaberg, where I was at the time, and there he collected a lot of money. It was unbelievable how this unlearned and unashamed monk could put on airs. He said that if a Christian slept with his own dear mother and then placed money in the pope's indulgence collection box, the pope had the power in heaven and on earth to forgive him, and when he had forgiven him, God himself had to grant forgiveness. If the people would plunk down their money right away and purchase grace and indulgence, then all the mountains around Saint Annaberg would yield nothing but pure silver. As soon as just one dime clanged in the collection box, the soul of the one for whom the offering was made would immediately fly off to heaven. This is the way he praised the indulgences. To put it briefly: our Lord God was no longer God but had given all divine power to the pope: you are Peter, to you I give the keys of heaven, and whatever you bind, etc. So the words *Petrus* [Peter] and *Petra* [rock], *clavis* [key] and *solvere* [to absolve] had to be interpreted to refer to the pope alone, and this inquisitor [Tetzel] wanted to excommunicate and burn anyone who contradicted him. The indulgence paper was so revered that when the money chest was brought into a town, the document was carried on a satin or golden cloth and all the priests, monks, town council members, students, men, women, and children met the indulgence with flags and candles, with singing in a procession. The bells were rung, the organ played, and it was accompanied into the church, where a cross was erected, the pope's banners were displayed, and, in short, God himself would not have gotten that kind of welcome.[1]

Pastor Mathesius, how did Luther get involved in the controversy over indulgences? In 1516 the indulgence drumbeater Johan Tetzel (for whom Elector Frederick of Saxony had entered a plea with Emperor Maximilian, who wanted him executed for adultery) was selling the Roman indulgence as the agent commissioned by several bishops who

---

1. Myconius, "Historia," 14.

desired to discharge their debts for their episcopal robes in Rome with the money gathered in German lands.[2]

What did that have to do with Luther? Doctor Luther, as a baptized member of the Christian church, had carried with him from his youth a desire and heartfelt longing for Holy Scripture and hoped to learn it in the cloister and attain to God's grace through it. He often told his hearers that he was assigned to become a doctor of Holy Scripture and because of this began to interpret Holy Scripture in the cloister and to dispute sophistry and to drive back the scholastics with their new four ways or sects . . . At this time, as he was setting forth new and firm principles and foundations of our Christian faith from God's Word and confessing them openly, that Holy Scripture alone shows us the way to heaven, Johann Tetzel was offering his indulgence junk in Jüterbog, thirty miles from Wittenberg. And this raging Roman peddler, like a real con artist and liar, gave speeches with huge claims. He said that his red cross with the pope's coat of arms was as powerful as the cross of Jesus Christ. He boasted that he did not want to meet Saint Peter in heaven because he had redeemed more souls with his indulgence than Saint Peter had with his gospel. He claimed that the grace of an indulgence was precisely the grace through which a person would be reconciled with God. He preached that reconciliation was to be had without lament, remorse, regret, or repentance for sins, when a person purchased his and the pope's letter bestowing grace. For as soon as the penny clunked in his money chest, the soul would make its way from purgatory to heaven. Such great grace and power had been bestowed upon him at Rome. Even if a person were to rape Mary, the mother of God, he

---

2. Mathesius, *Historien*, Xa.

could be forgiven of that along with future sins if he put the appropriate amount in the chest.[3]

What did Luther do in reaction to what he had heard about Tetzel's preaching? When Tetzel and his supporters with the Roman and episcopal authorization and the keys of the church were trying to defend their messing around, Doctor Luther was forced by his doctoral oath and his position as a teacher of the church to take positions against Johann Tetzel and all who lay under the same blanket. He nailed his theses on the Castle church door in Wittenberg on the festival of its namesake [All Saints] and had them published. They began, "Our Lord and master Jesus Christ said, 'repent, for the kingdom of heaven is at hand,' etc. [Matt. 4:17]" This is the first question of our Doctor regarding the Roman indulgence: do such indulgences for purchase forgive all punishment and guilt and redeem the soul from purgatory? Or, does this forgiveness take place through genuine Christian repentance and turning to God, when one regrets his sin from the heart and believes the holy absolution, that when a person trusts that only because of the matchless blood of Jesus Christ, out of pure grace, all his original and actual sins were forgiven, insofar as he has good intentions, so far as it is humanly possible with the power of the Holy Spirit, nevermore to sin and to enter into a new, holy life?[4]

Doctor Cochlaeus, how do you see the matter of Tetzel's preaching of Pope Leo's indulgence? Since Luther, who was adorned with the title of doctor and provost and was to be giving regular lectures in theology, was an extremely zealous debater and conceited, he desired to be the most prominent scholar and not just in Wittenberg. He went to Heidelberg, where he sought fame for his intelligence and learning in a

3. Mathesius, *Historien*, XIa–b.
4. Mathesius, *Historien*, XIIa–b.

The Media Revolution and the Thickets of Controversy

disputation in which he proposed new ideas. Then it happened that, in 1517, Pope Leo published new indulgences for the whole world because of the new construction of the Cathedral of Saint Peter in Rome, which his predecessor Pope Julius II had begun with the most splendid splendor. But Julius's death prevented him from completing this magnificent project. Pope Julius, a high-minded man, began to rebuild the old cathedral in the most gigantic, most impressive dimensions. Pope Leo, a generous man, more inclined to spending (I will not say squandering) funds rather than gathering and soliciting them, did not have sufficient resources of his own. Therefore, he issued the indulgences in order to gain the helping hands of many who would provide pious support. Furthermore, at this time there was a most prominent man, in regard to both his high dignity and the majesty of his birth, the Most Reverend father and most illustrious prince, Albrecht, archbishop of Mainz and Magdeburg, priest and cardinal of the Holy Roman church, primate of Germany and Elector Prince of the Holy Roman Empire, margrave of Brandenburg, etc. Therefore, Pope Leo X prepared a special commission for him to manage the business of publishing the indulgences in Germany.[5]

What was the chief issue that divided Tetzel and Luther, Doctor Cochlaeus? Luther began, "Our Lord and master Jesus Christ, by saying 'make your repentance, etc.' [Matt. 4:17] wanted to make the whole life of a believer to be one of repentance." That verse cannot be understood as referring to the penitential sacrament of confession and satisfaction, which is celebrated by the ministry of a priest, he said. But the word does not refer only to inner repentance. Indeed, the inner repentance is nothing unless it is manifested externally through various mortifications of the flesh, etc. In opposition to his opinion, Tetzel began as follows, "Our

5. Cochlaeus, *Historia*, 2a–3a; *Lives* 56.

Lord Jesus Christ not only desired everyone to be bound by the sacraments of the new law after his passion and ascension. He also desired to teach these sacraments to all after his passion through his extremely pointed preaching. He is in error, therefore, who says that Christ, when he preached, 'perform your repentance,' taught interior repentance and exterior mortification of the flesh but that he did not also wish to teach and to imply at the same time the sacrament of penance and its part of confession and satisfaction. They are obligatory. For indeed there is no benefit at all, even if the inner suffering accompanies outer mortification, unless there be present, also, in fact or by promise, confession and satisfaction, etc. Thus, through publishing propositions of divergent and contrary opinions, the controversy with its turbulent disagreement between these two antagonists appeared to be waged so publicly that in the next year it broke out into an open fire. It destroyed and dissolved the peace and unity of the church to the greatest offense of the weak and the detriment of souls. Luther trusted in his own intellect and learning and also in the power and favor of his protector, Duke Frederick the Elector, and in the advice and machinations of his wily Staupitz.[6]

Doctor Cochlaeus, how did Luther gain such a following after the publication of his theses on indulgences? Relying on the advice of his associates, he published a Latin book titled *Resolution of the Disputations concerning the Power of Indulgences, etc.* In that book he set forth ninety-five theses matching his new opinions, not, to be sure, so that he could reconcile himself with the pope and his adversaries or succeed in placating them. He attacked them most bitterly and extensively in this book itself because he wanted to enlist the reader's support for his own cause. He pretended to be humble, submissive, and respectful toward the Roman

6. Cochlaeus, *Historia*, 5a–b; *Luther's Lives*, 59.

pontiff. By this, he was cunningly seeking to elicit both the reader's sympathy for himself and hatred for his opponents. For he pretended that he was snatched and dragged into public view, entirely reluctant and unwilling, by his opponents' wickedness. He said in his preface addressed to Leo X, "Reluctantly I come into public discussion. I am especially unlearned and stupid in my thinking, and I lack scholarly abilities. But necessity drives me to squawk like a goose among swans. Therefore, in order to ameliorate my opponents and meet the wishes of many, I am publishing my trifles." Later he said, "Therefore, Most Holy Father, I offer myself prostrate at your most holy feet, with all that I am and all that I have. Give me life, kill me, summon me, reprove me, approve or disapprove, as it will please you. I recognize your voice as the voice of Christ, presiding and speaking in you. If I have deserved death, I will not refuse to die." So, by this cunning, as he complained that he was unjustly pressed by his opponents and driven into public view, he soon gained the most widespread favor for himself. That was so not only among the simple people, who easily believe and freely open their wide-open, itching ears to every innovation, but also among many serious, learned men. They believed in his words through genuine simplicity. They thought that this monk sought nothing else than the defense of the truth against the seekers of indulgences, who, according to Luther's repeated accusation, appeared more zealous for money than for souls. In order to deflect any suspicion of heresy from himself onto his opponents, he joined a certain solemn protestation to the book [*Resolution of the Disputations*], after his complaints to Staupitz and his letters to Pope Leo. In it he deferred not only to the Holy Scriptures but also to the holy canonical and pontifical decrees and the church fathers; moreover, he said he desired to consider the judgment of his superiors sound in all matters.[7]

Was Luther for the most part alone as he published his criticism of indulgences, Doctor Cochlaeus? Right away, a learned body of poets and rhetoricians [biblical humanists], who were also driven by hatred for his opponents, sympathized with Luther and argued enthusiastically in his behalf by speaking and by writing. They made his cause attractive to the laity. With all kinds of carping and insults they struck out at the prelates and theologians of the church, accusing them of avarice, pride, envy, barbarous behavior, and ignorance. They said that these churchmen were persecuting the innocent Luther for no reason other than his teaching, which seemed to them, and was, more scholarly and more conducive to speaking the truth than the sham and tricks of the hypocrites. The poets and rhetoricians were so strong not only in both their cleverness and their animosity but also in the elegance of their language, oral and written, that they easily drew the minds of the laity to favor and sympathize with Luther. They viewed him as one who was being harassed for the sake of truth and righteousness by the jealous, greedy, and unlearned while they believed that the churchmen lived in leisure and luxury and extorted money from the simple people by exploiting their superstitions.[8]

What impact did this have, Doctor Cochlaeus, on the indulgence offerings? Tetzel had been a good fundraiser and often preached indulgences. But now his authority decreased more and more each day among the populace due to these sorts of complaints by both Luther and the poets and rhetoricians. The enthusiasm of the people for indulgences declined, and those who collected the payments and the supervisors were seen as despicable. The gangs of

7. Cochlaeus, *Historia*, 6a; *Luther's Lives*, 60.
8. Cochlaeus, *Historia*, 6b–7a; *Luther's Lives*, 60–61.

corrupt officials became smaller. On the other hand, Luther's authority, favor, trust, esteem, and fame were all increasing since he appeared to be so open and judicious, one who powerfully asserted the truth against the deception of the money collectors and the empty promises of vaporous indulgence documents. For those who sold indulgences did not give them away for free but charged a good price for them. Meanwhile, at Rome Luther's opponents were procuring a citation by which Luther was called to trial before the papal court.[9]

Martin Bucer, some years before you became pastor in Strassburg, you heard Luther defend his theses on his "theology of the cross" at the Augustinian meeting in 1518. What were your impressions? Although our leading men refuted him with all their might, their wiles were not able to make him move an inch from his propositions. His pleasant manner of answering is remarkable; his patience in listening is incomparable. In his explanations you would recognize the acumen of Paul, not of Scotus. His answers, so brief, so wise, and drawn from the Holy Scriptures, easily made all his hearers his admirers. On the next day I had a face-to-face, friendly conversation with the man alone, and a supper rich with doctrine rather than with dainties. He lucidly explained whatever I might ask. He agrees with Erasmus in all things, but with this difference in his favor, that what Erasmus only insinuates, he teaches openly and freely. Would that I had time to convey more of this. He has brought it about that at Wittenberg the ordinary textbooks have all been abolished while the Greek fathers and Jerome, Augustine, and Paul are publicly taught.[10]

Doctor Cochlaeus, how did the conversation—or confrontation—between Cardinal Cajetan and Luther come to

9. Cochlaeus, *Historia*, 7a; *Luther's Lives*, 61.
10. Bucer, *Correspondance*, 1:82.

an end? The legate readily understood that Luther's answers were mere words, and he was still holding in his mind his errors and opinions. Therefore, the legate said to him that unless he recanted, he would be handed over to the officers in accord with the pope's command, to be bound [to be taken to Rome]. Luther had heard that the legate had a mandate for seizing and jailing both him and his comrade Staupitz. For this reason, he was very afraid. Since he was forbidden to return into the legate's sight unless he recanted, he began secretly to seek a safe conduct through friends who were members of the imperial household. When this was accomplished, supported by the advice of his friend Staupitz, he wrote an appeal, challenging the legate to inform the pope in better fashion. He ordered that this appeal be made public after he had secretly left Augsburg in order to stir up the majority of the people against the pope and legate and more hatred of them among the laity.[11]

Peter Mosellanus, as an instructor in Leipzig and a recorder of Luther's debate with Johann Eck in 1519, what impressions did you carry away from your conversations with him? Martin is of medium height with a gaunt body that has been so exhausted by studies and worries that one can almost count the bones under his skin: yet he is manly and vigorous with a high clear voice. He is full of learning and has an excellent knowledge of the Scriptures, so that he can refer to facts as if they were at his fingertips . . . In his life and behavior, he is very courteous and friendly, and there is nothing of the stern stoic or grumpy fellow about him. He can adjust to all occasions. In a social gathering he is gay, witty, ever full of joy, always has a bright and happy face, no matter how seriously his adversaries threaten him.

---

11. Cochlaeus, *Historia* 8b; *Luther's Lives*, 62.

One can see that God's strength is with him in his difficult undertaking...[12]

Pastor Myconius, what did you hear about the Leipzig Debate? Eck cited many of the Fathers, glosses on texts, interpretations, canons from Councils, but Luther quoted Scripture and the ancient fathers. There were notaries who recorded everything. The proceedings were published; people can read them. Eck was treated royally wherever he went.... From that day on, Eck persevered as an enemy and persecutor of the gospel, to this very day, and he is arousing the dukes of Bavaria, King Ferdinand, the bishops (whose only idol he is), and whomever he can against the gospel.[13]

Doctor Luther, what happened when you went to Leipzig to debate with Johannes Eck? Almost at the very moment of our arrival, even before we had gotten out of our wagon, a document issued by the bishop of Merseburg was nailed to the doors of the churches, forbidding the debate, with a newly published papal explanation concerning this matter of indulgences. This document was ignored, and the person who had posted it was thrown into jail by the city council because he had acted without its knowledge. Since our enemies got nowhere with this trick, they tried another. They called Andreas Karlstadt to meet alone with them and tried hard to get him to hold the debate orally, according to Eck's wishes, without stenographers taking down the proceedings in writing. Eck hoped that he might carry off the victory by his loud shouting and impressive delivery. He had long used such methods to his advantage. Karlstadt, however, opposed this and insisted that they proceed according to what had been previously agreed, that is, that the statements of the disputants be written down by stenographers. To attain this, he was compelled to agree

12. Hoppe, ed., *Luthers Sämtliche Schriften*, 15:1200–201.
13. Myconius, "Historia," 35.

that the account of the debate made by the stenographers should not be published prior to a hearing by a court of judges. At this point a new dispute arose over the choice of judges. At length they compelled him also to consent to postpone coming to an agreement concerning the judges until after the debate had been concluded . . . The next day they called me to appear before them and proposed the same thing. Suspecting, however, the pope as the instigator of this procedure, I refused to accept these conditions. My colleagues had persuaded me to do so. Then they proposed other universities as judges, without the pope. I requested that the freedom upon which we had earlier agreed be honored. When they were unwilling to do this, I became reluctant and was ready to give up on the debate. Then the rumor spread that I did not want to risk participating in the debate and, what was particularly unfair, that I wished to have no judges.[14]

Doctor Luther, what were the chief issues that you debated with Eck? Eck debated with me, at first very acrimoniously, concerning the primacy of the pope. His proof rested on the words "You are Peter . . ." [Matt 16:18] and "feed my sheep . . . follow me" [John 21:17, 22] and "strengthen your brothers" [Luke 22:32], adding to these passages many quotations from the church fathers. . . . Then, coming to the last point, he rested his case entirely on the Council of Constance, which had condemned Hus's article alleging that papal authority derived from the emperor instead of from God. Then Eck stomped about with much ado as though he were in an arena, holding up the Bohemians [Jan Hus and his supporters] before me and publicly accusing me of the heresy of the Bohemian heretics and supporting them. He is a sophist, no less impudent than rash. These accusations tickled the Leipzig audience more than the

14. WA Br 1:421; LW 31:319–20.

substance of the debate itself. In rebuttal, I mentioned the Greek Christians for the past thousand years and also the ancient church fathers who had not been under the authority of the Roman pontiff although I did not deny the primacy of honor due the pope. Finally, we also debated the authority of a council. I publicly acknowledged that some articles had been wrongly condemned by the Council of Constance, articles which had been taught in plain and clear words by Paul, Augustine, and even Christ himself. At this point that snake swelled up, exaggerated my crime, and nearly went insane in praising his hearers there in Leipzig. I proved by the words of the council itself that not all the articles that it condemned were actually heretical and erroneous. So Eck's proofs had accomplished nothing. There the matter rested. The third week Eck and I debated penance, purgatory, indulgences, and the power of a priest to grant absolution. Eck did not like to debate with Karlstadt and asked me to debate alone with him. The debate over indulgences fell completely flat, for Eck agreed with me in nearly all respects. His former defense of indulgences came to appear like mockery and derision, whereas I had hoped that this would be the main topic of the debate . . .[15]

Doctor Luther, your treatises setting forth the central concerns you had about the state of the church were not only in Latin, for the clergy, but also in part in German. How do you explain taking these topics to the crowd, to the common people? Although I know full well and hear every day that many people think little of me and say that I only write little pamphlets and sermons in German for the uneducated laity, I do not let that stop me. Would to God that in my lifetime I had, to my fullest ability, helped one layperson to be better! I would be quite satisfied, thank God, and quite willing then to let all my little books perish. Whether

15. WA Br 1:421; LW 31:321–22.

the making of many large books is an art and of benefit to Christendom I leave for others to judge. But I believe that if I were of a mind to write big books of their kind, I could perhaps, with God's help, do it more readily than they could write my kind of little discourse. . . . I will not be ashamed in the slightest to preach to the uneducated laypeople and write for them in German. Although I may have little skill at it myself, it seems to me that if we had hitherto busied ourselves in this very task and were of a mind to do more of it in the future, Christendom would have reaped no small advantage. Christians would have been more benefitted by this than by those heavy, weighty tomes and those *questions*, which are only handled in the schools among learned schoolmen.[16]

Pastor Mathesius, when did you encounter Luther's classic presentations of his teaching in the great treatises of 1520–1522? In 1520 the fine Christian book *On Good Works* was issued. I learned of it in 1526, praise God, in Bavaria at the Odelzhausen Castle. Along with this work, because Doctor Eck had helped Luther confirm that the Roman curia was the true Babylon, in which the true Antichrist was holding holy Christendom captive with his decrees, idolatry, and orders, with his baseless disputations and useless books, Luther wrote on excommunication and on the Babylonian captivity of the church. He attacked the entire new Roman religion and the worship it fabricated according to human reason. He taught that Jesus Christ had instituted the entire Lord's Supper with the Christian plea that a place be made for the reintroduction of the entire Supper of the true body and blood of the Lord for the bride of Jesus Christ, and of the proper Christian mass together with the proper

---

16. WA 6:203; LW 44:22.

distribution of the Lord's Supper. With these treatises Doctor Luther ignited a new fire.[17]

DISCUSSION QUESTIONS

1. Describe Johannes Tetzel. Was he a hero, a villain, a victim in the unfolding story of the Wittenberg Reformation?
2. Why did the issue of indulgences not assume a larger role than it did in the ongoing debate between Luther and his opponents?
3. Why did the issue of the papacy's authority loom so large so quickly in their dispute?
4. Compare and contrast Luther and Johannes Eck in terms of personality and theological position.
5. Was Luther justified in taking his concerns to the general public by writing in German, or should he have confined himself to the educated theologians and only published in Latin?

FURTHER READING

1. The biographies and overviews of Luther's theology listed in the introduction.
2. Edwards, Mark U., Jr., *Printing, Propaganda, and Martin Luther*. 1994. Reprint, Minneapolis: Fortress, 2004.
3. Pettegree, Andrew. *Brand Luther: 1517, Printing, and the Making of the Reformation.* New York: Penguin, 2015.

---

17. Mathesius, *Historien*, XVIIb–XIXa.

4. Wengert, Timothy J. *Martin Luther's Ninety-Five Theses: With Introduction, Commentary, and Study Guide.* Minneapolis: Fortress, 2015.

5. Bagchi, David V. N. *Luther's Earliest Opponents: Catholic Controversialists, 1518–1525.* Minneapolis: Fortress, 1991.

Chapter 5

Worms, the Wartburg, and Wittenberg

THE PROCLAMATION OF THE papal bull threatening excommunication and that which fulfilled the threat challenged Eck's imagination. Pope Leo had commissioned him to distribute first the warning and then the condemnation. Eck recognized that his life could be in danger from an angry populace in some places. He found a substitute to convey the bull to Wittenberg. That was probably best for all concerned. The students displayed no patience at all with papal political machinations nor with those defending what they considered the old, decrepit, corrupt system. They burned copies of the bull threatening excommunication, *Exsurge, Domine*, on December 20, 1520. Although no professors were prepared to give up their copies of the works of scholastic theologians, canon law books went onto the flames as well. The arrival of the actual condemnation in *Decet pontificum Romanum* was anticlimactic.

Negotiations went on between electoral Saxon and imperial officials. In 1520 Emperor Charles V assumed office, succeeding his grandfather Emperor Maximilian, duke of Austria, of the Habsburg family. The Habsburgs did use military force when necessary to further the family's interests, but Maximilian had shrewdly extended his power and that of his house by marriages. He married Mary of Burgundy, heir to the lands of this dukedom at the western edge of French domains that had fallen in the fourteenth century to the family of Philip the Bold. The French king assumed rule of the southern part of the principality at the death of Mary's father, but she brought the Low Countries with her into her marriage, one of the earliest industrial centers in medieval Europe and thus a land of great wealth. Mary and Maximilian expanded the power of the family by marrying their son Philip to Joanna, daughter of the two monarchs ruling most of the Iberian peninsula, Ferdinand, king of Aragon, and Isabella, queen of Leon and Castile. Charles inherited not only extensive lands in southern Germany and the Low Countries but also the Iberian, Italian, and American domains that should have fallen to his mother (Iberian law recognized the right of women to rule) had she not been confined to a cloister, probably for political reasons though she was said to be insane. Charles's sister Mary extended family claims to Bohemia and Hungary with her marriage to King Ladislaus (Louis) II. Upon his death in 1526 battling invading Turkish forces, Charles assumed those thrones, with Mary as regent.

Charles reigned over more territory in Europe than any other individual between Charlemagne and Napoleon. In fact, that extensive claim to power weakened his hand within his German Empire considerably. His enemies included the French monarchy under Francis I; the restless nobility in Iberia, who resisted (in vain) his efforts to amalgamate Aragon with Castile and Leon; pirates on the Mediterranean; at times the pope himself; and above all, the Turks. The Ottoman Empire had been on the move for more than two centuries. In 1529 its advance into Europe was halted at the gates of Charles's German "capital," Vienna, after a bloody, gruesome siege.

Charles had been raised in Flanders. His tutor, Adriaan Floriszn Boeyens (1459–1523), professor of theology at Leuven, later served Charles as regent for his Iberian realms and was elected pope in 1522. Boeyens conveyed to the young prince the concern for reform and the pious devotion that Erasmus typified, and that embodied the spirit of the Brethren of the Common Life, a lay semimonastic movement that had arisen in the Netherlands in the fourteenth century. Charles sought reform of ecclesiastical practice, but only in regard to moral standards, especially of the clergy, and institutional forms. He had no understanding of Luther's doctrinal and pastoral concerns. He perceived any challenge to authority, and particularly to papal authority, which held his world together (except when it challenged princely authority), as more than dangerous. Therefore, he was not inclined to favor Luther's person or call to reform in any way. But the support of Frederick the Wise, the first cousin once removed of his grandfather, had played a critical role in Charles's victory over Francis I of France in his election to the imperial throne. Therefore, Charles resisted the pressure from Girolamo Aleander, papal legate in the Empire, and agreed to summon Luther to the imperial diet scheduled to meet in Worms in the spring of 1521.

Luther knew well that Jan Hus had received a safe conduct to come to the Council of Constance from Charles's predecessor as emperor, Sigismund, in 1414, and that the council had decided that heretics had no right to a safe conduct. Hus and his supporter, Jerome of Prague, were burned at the stake before the council concluded. Nonetheless, Luther said that even if there were as many demons as roof tiles in Worms, he would go to appear before the princes and imperial town council representatives assembled there for the diet.

He entered the city to the sound of trumpets and received the same adulation he had been given by crowds along the way, in town after town. That did not alter the fierce determination of Aleander and other advisors of the emperor to quash the heretic and end the heretical movement. Aleander's reports reveal his vexation and frustration at seeing Luther's portrait and publications being sold throughout Worms. Hearing exaggerated praise for the Wittenberg professor from people at all levels of society disgusted the Italian diplomat. Aleander pressed the emperor incessantly to end the entire affair by arresting Luther and sending him to the stake. Charles decided not to risk either princely antagonism or popular discontent, possibly revolt. Against his will, the emperor reluctantly permitted the smelter's son to appear before the diet to recant.

With fear and trepidation Luther came before the diet on April 17, 1521. He had never met with Elector Frederick, to say nothing of other princes. Fearless criticism of men of higher station that later typified his public utterances had not yet germinated in his disposition. He was somewhat surprised when he was not asked to explain his plans for reform. Instead, an official of the archbishop of Trier, also named Johannes Eck, representing the imperial government, asked him if the publications laid out on a table came from his pen. Luther asked for the titles to be read and then claimed them as his own. Eck demanded rejection of their content. Luther asked for time to consider his answer. Eck expressed indignation at the request but granted him a day. That evening visitors dropped by Luther's lodging to encourage him.

April 18 brought him before the diet again. He distinguished three groups among his writings: 1) works of edification and devotion, cultivating piety, with which no one should find fault; 2) works criticizing abuses in practice and false teaching; to retract them would only promote godlessness; 3) works condemning positions of individuals. In regard to the last category Luther conceded that he had spoken too harshly at times, but because he saw them as defenses of the honor and teaching of Christ, he was not prepared to go against Scripture, rational argumentation, and his "conscience" (which he understood as his entire disposition or orientation toward God and life), since this conscience was captive to God's Word. Accounts of the time, including Luther's own, do not mention the words "here I stand, I cannot do anything else," although that phrase captures what the Wittenberg professor was actually doing.

Though the Spanish soldiers whom Charles had brought to Worms threatened Luther, the populace acclaimed him as their hero. Charles had as much fear as Luther of what might happen in the ensuing days, though the emperor feared popular revolt and princely rebellion whereas the professor feared the heretic's pyre. Negotiations and conversations continued for several days. Luther left Worms on April 26, accompanied by an imperial herald who guaranteed his safe conduct. The diet adjourned, and Charles assembled a group of princes he knew he could count on to approve his edict ordering the eradication of the Lutheran heresy and the execution of the reformer and his followers who refused to submit to papal obedience. He predated the edict so that it would appear accepted while the diet was officially still in session. Anyone who could deliver Luther dead or alive would win the acclaim of both pope and emperor.

The imperial herald was dismissed by Luther and his traveling companions, including by his colleague Nikolaus von Amsdorf. Soon thereafter, on May 4, men on horseback stopped the wagon transporting them and seized Luther. Amsdorf and Luther had at least some sense that something like this was going to happen; the other two or three in the party were terrified. The reformer disappeared.

Frederick the Wise stood behind the kidnapping, although he himself probably did not know the details. His advisor, Luther's friend Georg Spalatin, did. Spalatin had served as the go-between for the prince and the professor for several years at this point. He remained Luther's channel to and from the world outside the Wartburg castle, to which his kidnappers took him. The Wartburg overlooked Eisenach and his old school. There the castellan provided generously for "Junker Jörg," as Luther was dubbed. Inactivity plagued him and produced stomach problems and other ailments. Nonetheless, Luther's ten months there, from May 1521 to February 1522, proved to be one of the most productive times of his life.

He recognized the need for several tools to implement reform. By this time he knew the power of the printing press in aiding this implementation. Priests who wanted to make their sermons the center of the congregation's life did not know how to preach, so Luther prepared the first of his sermon collections for them. This genre was labeled a "postil." Luther often criticized the postils of the late Middle Ages for two reasons. First, they made for lazy preachers, who did not need to prepare their own sermons. Second, they contained chiefly encouragement for earning one's salvation through good works, or merely recited legends of the saints with fictional accounts of their superhuman powers. In these months he also wrote several other treatises deconstructing papal claims to divinely granted power over the church and monastic claims to a holier way of life.

Worms, the Wartburg, and Wittenberg

In Wittenberg Melanchthon and Amsdorf were supposed to be in charge, but Karlstadt thought of himself as the senior among the Wittenberg reformers. With the enthusiastic support of Gabriel Zwilling, one of Luther's Augustinian brothers, he sped to introduce practical reforms. Minor iconoclastic incidents took place. Luther slipped back into town to assess the situation in December 1521 and decided that his colleagues could get along without his help. On this occasion he and Melanchthon discussed the need for a new German translation of the Bible. Luther resolved to undertake the project.

In eleven weeks a translation of the New Testament was ready to be sent to the printers. This was not the first appearance of the words of Scripture in German. About twenty German translations existed already. All were based on the Vulgate, the Latin translation dating back to Jerome eleven hundred years earlier. None had been produced by people with Luther's gift of hearing the music of the German language. Luther too depended first of all upon the Latin Vulgate, which he had heard and read all his life. But he turned as well to Erasmus's edition of the Greek text and usually (though not in every case) followed it when the Vulgate deviated from it. Luther had practiced translation as he prepared sermons and other materials in the previous years. In 1522 he focused on formulating the evangelists' and apostles' words in the language that he heard on the streets.

Although some have exaggerated his role in shaping modern German, his crucial contribution to the development of the language and literature of the German-speaking peoples cannot be ignored. His rendering of biblical phrases implanted new expressions in German speech and in the speech of other languages whose own vernacular translations followed Luther's lead. Many of these phrases are commonplace to this day. Although Luther emphasized the oral proclamation of God's Word on the basis of Scripture, he also provided models for reading Holy Scripture, he counseled a combination of prayer [*oratio*] and meditation [*meditatio*] within the context of the believer's spiritual struggles [*tentatio*] with temptations of all kinds as the ideal approach to digesting the Bible's message.

Meanwhile, in Wittenberg restlessness was on the rise. On December 25, 1521, Karlstadt celebrated the Lord's Supper, distributing the blood of Christ as well as his body to the people, in defiance of roughly four hundred years' custom. Many laypeople were uncomfortable with this innovation, as was Frederick the Wise (although he would commune "in both kinds" on his deathbed four years later). As reports of rising disquiet in Wittenberg reached the Wartburg, "Junker Jörg" decided it was time to return to his cloister. In Invocavit week 1522 (the week following the first Sunday in Lent), March 8–15, he preached a series of sermons in Wittenberg's town church, pleading for patience with weak consciences. Luther's dampening of the pace of change brought Zwilling back to his side, and he remained a faithful supporter of Luther into his Torgau pastorate and into old age.

Karlstadt, however, grew increasingly frustrated with Luther. Karlstadt's vision included many features of a profile of revolt and reform within the medieval church. Though none found solid footing, small movements had arisen time and time again in preceding centuries, advocating a *biblicism* that rejected many ecclesiastical traditions and practices, a *moralism* that advocated the imitation of Christ's ethical example rather than observance of sacred rituals, *anticlerical* and *antisacramental* tendencies, and often also a *millennialist* view of history that promised Christ's return and deliverance from ecclesiastical and social ills. Karlstadt rejected and condemned university learning and retreated to the parish in Orlamünde that had supported his professorship. His disapproval of Luther's emphasis on justification by faith alone and his colleague's understanding of Christ's presence in the Lord's Supper sparked ongoing controversy. Luther's feeling of betrayal by someone who should have known better fueled their dispute.

Spalatin continued to provide a bridge to the elector for Luther. Frederick remained steadfast in his silent support for Luther though he personally continued many of his earlier forms of piety, apart from displaying his relic collection each All Saints' Day. Luther kept a low profile during the next three years, preaching in the period when the town church pastor, Simon Heins, became ever more unable to exercise his duties before Johannes Bugenhagen assumed that office. Bugenhagen came from his monastic home in Pomerania, intrigued by Luther's *Babylonian Captivity of the Church*, and quickly entered the circle around him. Luther finally began formal teaching again, first on Deuteronomy in the Black Cloister in 1523–1524, and then officially for the university with lectures on the Minor Prophets in 1525.

Larger social issues attracted Luther's attention when they involved the exercise of God's callings in home, occupation, society, and the congregation. In 1524, *On Trade and Usury*, his critique of business practices and budding capitalistic procedures called on believers to adhere to God's command to love neighbors and serve their needs. He addressed members of town councils in 1524, calling on them to support schooling for boys and girls in order to provide for leadership in church and society. His *Sermon on Keeping Children in School* (1530) issued a similar admonition to parents to support their children's learning. A series of treatises on legal matters relating to marriage complemented his encouragement of good parenting and love for spouses in sermons and devotional treatises. Because he believed that physical or political compulsion could not change inner convictions, Luther opposed the execution of heretics. He also rejected the papal call for a crusade against the Turks in order to regain the lands they had conquered with their jihad. His call for imperial protection against the invading Ottoman armies was coupled with a rejection of the concept of a religious crusade in several treatises, including *On War against the Turks* (1529).

In 1521 and 1522 Luther's altercation with King Henry VIII over the sacraments typified his growing willingness to criticize political powers. The king had written, with perhaps some help from clerical advisors, a sharp critique of Luther's *On the Babylonian Captivity of the Church*, his deconstruction of medieval sacramental doctrine and practice. Luther answered in kind, as he did when Duke Georg of Saxony published his rejoinders to what he regarded as Luther's heretical teachings. Luther urged his students not to spare the unjust practices of rulers and courtiers in their sermons. If they did, he concluded, they would be as guilty as those public officials of fostering rebellion in the oppressed, exploited common people.

In the years following Luther's return, the team around him in Wittenberg changed. Amsdorf left on amicable terms to lead the reform of the church in Magdeburg, and Karlstadt left on less than amicable terms. Not only Bugenhagen joined the instructors of theology at the university; Justus Jonas came from Erfurt in 1521 to teach canon law, although the reform of the curriculum to focus on lectures on Scripture led him to abandon canon law for biblical interpretation in 1522. All of them worked closely with Wittenberg printers and those in other towns.

The years 1522–1525 brought Luther success as his measures for reform were introduced in towns and territories to one extent or another. Pressure from the imperial government continued. At the diet called to Nuremberg in 1523, a compromise formula permitted each territorial government to have the gospel preached in its lands until a general council could, within a year, determine proper teaching. "Gospel" was not defined, although the imperial will to suppress reform was clear. The next year the diet followed the lead of Charles V in repeating the condemnations of the Edict of Worms. Such measures did not stop those who still claimed to be under their bishops and ultimately the Holy Father in Rome from making the significant alterations in preaching and practice that followed and implemented Luther's call for reform.

INTERVIEWS

Pastor Spalatin, you were Elector Frederick's closest advisor at the time. Did the elector think a whole lot about what to do in regard to Luther? You have mentioned that he consulted Erasmus, for instance, on what he should be doing. In 1520, on November 5, as the Roman emperor Charles V had received the royal Roman crown in Aachen and moved on to Cologne, Elector Frederick of praiseworthy and blessed memory gave Erasmus of Rotterdam an urgent invitation to come to his electoral grace where he was staying on the square of the Holy Three Kings. He graciously received him and had a conversation with him, back and forth, in my presence, in the grand hall, in front of the fireplace. Although my most gracious lord, Duke Frederick of Saxony, the Elector, would have much preferred that Rotterdam speak in Low German, he did not get his way. Rotterdam stuck with his Latin, for which he set such a standard above thousands of others that it was very understandable, good Latin, loud and clear. Therefore, my highly respected

Elector of Saxony, Duke Frederick, understood him and replied, his electoral grace commanding me each time how I should answer Rotterdam. Through me his electoral grace asked Rotterdam if he thought what Doctor Martin Luther had taught, preached, and written to that point was in error. Rotterdam first smacked his lips before he gave his answer. Then my gracious lord, Duke Frederick of Saxony, closed his eyes, as was his manner when he expected a reliable answer from the people with whom he was talking. Then Erasmus of Rotterdam sat up and said clearly in Latin, "Luther has sinned in two ways, namely, he struck the crown of the pope and the bellies of the monks." That was the answer Erasmus of Rotterdam gave the elector of Saxony regarding Doctor Martin Luther. Sometime later, barely two years before his death, his electoral grace said to me at his castle in Lochau, "When a person reads Rotterdam's writings and books for a longer time, he does not know what to expect." That was true, for there is nothing in them that is certain, upon which the conscience can build, neither for life nor for death. In the days after this conversation, Erasmus of Rotterdam was so well disposed to the teaching of Doctor Martin Luther that as I walked with him to the residence of the Count of Newenar, provost in Cologne, he changed his mind and wrote out in Latin some axiomata, as he called them. They were short sentences, and gave them to me, written in his hand. Soon thereafter, however, Rotterdam wrote to me with the urgent request that I should send the manuscript back to him. Hieronymus Aleander, papal legate at that time, could have used them to make difficulties for him. So fearful was Rotterdam of confessing Christian truth.[1]

Doctor Luther, what were your thoughts as you contemplated going to the Diet at Worms? At the time I perceived

1. Spalatin, "Annales," 29–30.

that they did not have any argument against me other than that I, in their opinion, had written against the practices and traditions of the church. I was not going to retract anything! I decided to answer Emperor Charles that I would not have come to Worms if I had been invited only so that I could recant. That would be the same as if I had gone and had returned already. If I had to do nothing but retract, then I could have done that from Wittenberg as well. If, however, he had invited me in order to kill me and because of my reaction he would see me as an enemy of the empire, then I was prepared to come. Because with Christ's help, I did not want to flee from conflict or abandon God's Word. I was quite certain that those bloodhounds would not rest until they had killed me. I wanted the papists to take the guilt of my blood upon themselves if only I could have accomplished that. It was clear that we had been made into pagans as we had been before Christ came. In this way the scheming Antichrist had held kingdoms imprisoned in his hands for centuries.[2]

We know that you were asked to recant three different types of books that you had written. After you had been granted a night to think over your answer, you distinguished between those you believed even your foes would have to approve since they were straightforward in their biblical teaching, those that attacked the papacy and its abuses, and those that criticized individuals—admitting that some of them may have been too harsh. How did you react? First, I said to the emperor and the assembly that "because I am a man and not God, I am not able to shield my books with any other protection than that which my Lord Jesus Christ himself offered for his teaching. When questioned before Annas about his teaching and struck by a servant, he said, 'if I have spoken wrongly, bear witness to the wrong' [John

2. WA BR 2:289, Nr. 389.

18:19–23]. If the Lord himself, who knew that he could not err, did not refuse to hear objections to his teaching, even from the lowest servant, how much more should I, who am the lowest scum and able to do nothing except err, desire and expect that someone should want to object to my teaching. Therefore, I ask by the mercy of God, may your most serene majesty, most illustrious lordships, or anyone at all who is able, either high or low, bear witness, expose my errors, overthrowing them by the writings of the prophets and evangelists. Once I have been so instructed, I shall be quite ready to renounce every error, and I shall be the first to cast my books into the fire."[3]

But you were not convinced that you were in error? No, and so I concluded, "Since then your serene majesty and your lordships seek a simple answer, I will give it in this manner, with neither horns nor teeth. Unless I am convinced by the testimony of the Scriptures or by clear reason (for I do not trust either in the pope or in councils alone since it is well known that they have often erred and contradicted each other), I am bound by the Scriptures that I have quoted, and my conscience is captive to God's Word. I cannot and I will not retract anything since it is neither safe nor right to go against conscience. May God help me. Amen."[4]

Six days later, you were summoned before Archbishop Richard of Trier. The chancellor of Baden, Hieronymus Vehus, attempted to convince you to recant. What was his argument? He said, that although the councils had set forth varying views, they did not contradict one another. Even if the councils had erred greatly, they had certainly not thereby destroyed their authority to such a degree that anyone would want to rely on his own interpretation in opposition to them. . . . He said that the church was not able to exist

3. WA 7:834; LW 32:111.
4. WA 7:835; LW 32:112.

without human institutions. The tree is known by its fruit [Matt. 12:33]. Moreover, it is said that many good things are the result of their laws. And Saint Martin, Saint Nicholas, and many other saints had taken part in councils. In addition, he said that my books would arouse great disorder and unbelievable confusion. The common people, he said, were using my book *The Freedom of a Christian* to throw off the yoke and to strengthen disobedience. "Now we are in a far different time from the time when those who believed were of one heart and soul [Acts 4:32]. Therefore, laws are necessary. Indeed, it must be recognized that although Luther has written many good things, and without doubt with a fine spirit, such as *On the Three Kinds of Righteousness* and others, the devil is using this fact and working through secret snares so that all Luther's works will be condemned . . ."[5]

How did you respond? I said, "I thank you as humbly as I am able for your merciful and kind disposition toward me which produced this admonition. I know that I am by far too lowly a person to deserve a warning from such great princes. I have not censured all councils but only that of Constance for the very powerful reason that it condemned God's Word, which is clear from its condemnation of the proposition of Jan Hus that the church of Christ is the community of the elect. . . . I will not refuse to pay with my life and blood rather than to be compelled to retract the clear Word of God."[6]

You then were sent away, and when you were called back to the assembly you were urged to place yourself under the emperor's judgment. How did you react? I said, "I will not and will never let it be said that I have dodged the judgment of the emperor, the princes, and the nobility of the empire.

5. WA 7:844–45; LW 32:116–17.
6. WA 7:845; LW 32:117.

I am so far from scorning their judgment that I will permit my works to be examined in detail and critically, so long as it is done on the authority of Holy Scripture and God's Word. For that Word is so clear to me that I am unable to yield unless taught better by God's Word."[7]

Superintendent Rhegius, what were your impressions after reports on Luther's appearance at the Diet of Worms arrived in Augsburg? You should know that Doctor Martin Luther is a real theologian, a real teacher of Scripture, to whom God's way of thinking, as it is in the Scripture, has been clearly revealed. For he looks at Scripture not darkly as through a glass made from temporal study or philosophy, as has been the case with the misinterpretation of the last more than three hundred years. He looks at them with a free, unencumbered perspective, with clear eyes, and therefore he sees them in their natural colors. He works at them in their original sense and understands them in the spirit in which they were written. That spirit will never be discovered to be more faithful to the Scriptures and lively than in the writings which he himself has written, which dissect the prophets and apostles as they thought and wrote. Therefore, you have to listen to Luther not with ears of the flesh, for what he says has not been revealed to blood and flesh but by the Spirit of God, for he speaks in the natural, real meaning of Scripture itself.[8]

Doctor Luther, how and when did you decide to be a reformer? I was not aware of it, but God was pushing me into working with the gospel. If I had known everything beforehand what I now know from experience, I would not have allowed myself to be pushed. But God's wisdom is greater than human wisdom. He simply blinded me as you would put blinders on a horse that must run a race.

7. WA 7:846; LW 32:118.
8. Rhegius, *Anzeigung,* d1b–d2a.

Therefore, when I began this, with intense seriousness and passionate commitment, I told God in my little cell that if he wanted to play a game with me, then he would do that for himself, but that he should keep me from letting myself, that is to say, letting my own wisdom, play along. He has powerfully heard this prayer.[9]

Pastor Spangenberg, how beneficial is Luther's translation of the Bible? Through Doctor Luther, as a tool that God took in hand, the Bible, the writings of the precious prophets and apostles, came into real, good, understandable German. That is an indescribable blessing, that the Holy Spirit has come to us Germans in these last days and has enunciated the great and sublime mysteries of God in German as clearly as he spoke in Hebrew and Greek. This translation of the Bible is a sublime divine effort, which all those who know the Hebrew language and the most learned among the Jews themselves have to respect highly. . . . It is undeniable that before the time of Luther the German language was corrupt, obscure, abstruse, and hard to understand. He brought back the real way of using the German language and established it in its purity and elegance. So we and all those who have come after him rightfully praise him as a father of the German language.[10]

Pastor Spalatin, did things settle down after Luther's return from the Wartburg? In 1523 the gospel and the whole religious cause came under attack. The Roman emperor, Charles, wrote to Duke Frederick of Saxony, the elector, from Spain, that the Lutheran teaching, described in the worst possible terms, had to be smothered and wiped out. Also in 1523 the prince of this world used the Bishop of Olmütz to move against God's Word and the cause of religion. He got King Louis of Hungary and Bohemia to issue

9. WA TR 1:601, Nr. 1206.

10. Spangenberg, *Warhafftiger Bericht*, C5a–C6a.

a public edict condemning Doctor Martinus's teaching as unchristian and ordering the burning of his books. This was implemented against the pure Christian, comforting teaching everywhere.[11]

Brother Murner, how do you assess Luther's calling for reform? Wherever there is a place where the devil and false teaching, of which the devil is the father, in some form or another are recognizable, that is a place that everyone would without doubt avoid and flee. Therefore, it is characteristic of such false teaching that it transforms and alters itself into forms with the appearance of proper terms and titles and does not permit me to recognize the little errors that have been used in addressing me. In doing just that, Doctor Luther or his learned followers obscured matters so that only skilled people can understand and see through what they are saying. They should have used these skills to promote the faith and the truth and given all of Christendom a cause for joy and praise. Instead of doing that, they misused the noble gifts of God, so that they can justly be compared to a madman who takes the sword in hand and harms and wounds himself and those around him. I received among other such booklets one that defended Doctor Martin Luther's booklet by a person who called himself a lover of God's truth. This author drew together a number of arguments to defend and advocate the Doctor's teaching and preaching. He regarded himself as Doctor Luther's disciple, and he was not ashamed of this but laid out the reasons that moved him to adhere to Luther in a proper godly reading. Luther was supposed to be like a Daniel whom God had raised up to protect the honorable Susanna (that is, the Christian church) against the villain from Babylon; and many similar thoughtless and presumptuous outrageous words without any foundation, according to this defense.... Now I intend

11. Spalatin, "Annales," 70–71.

to discharge my obligation to lift the sword against this master of fencing and apologist and turn it against him. First, he should know that the office of teaching, to fortify the faith, did not belong to him but to the councils and the whole of Christendom. As Saint Augustine said, he would not believe the gospel if it were not tested and approved by a council. [So I addressed this author], "Therefore, you, who have wrongly undertaken to confirm Doctor Luther's teaching, you have defended Doctor Luther's teaching in a faulty manner, and your blabbering and argumentation will not persuade or move anyone to accept Doctor Luther's teaching as believable. Proving something has two parts, and you have put forth the argument but not tested it. We could have let all your talk just be an air bubble, left it for what it was worth, and not examined it, had you not praised it and claimed that you had proven everything as true and that we wrongly had put down Doctor Martin's teaching. So, in view of these arguments that you put forth for our and many others' acceptance of such teaching, we will not accept them until they are tested by the entire Christian church and recognized as true—until the poison is taken out of the sugar."[12]

DISCUSSION QUESTIONS

1. Compare and contrast the concerns motivating Luther and those shaping Emperor Charles's view of Luther.
2. Why did Luther's appearance before the emperor so capture the popular imagination?
3. What was the importance of Luther's translation of the New Testament?

12. Murner, *Kleine Schriften* 1:120–21.

4. Was it wise for Luther to return to Wittenberg from the Wartburg when he did, or would it have been better if he had stayed in hiding?

5. What personal and theological factors contributed to the dissonance between Luther and Karlstadt?

FURTHER READING

1. The biographies and overviews of Luther's theology listed in the introduction.

2. Bluhm, Heinz. *Martin Luther, Creative Translator*. Saint Louis: Concordia, 1965.

3. Kolb, Robert. *Martin Luther and the Enduring Word of God: The Wittenberg School and Its Scripture-Centered Proclamation*. Grand Rapids: Baker Academic, 2016.

4. Bornkamm, Heinrich. *Luther in Mid-Career, 1521–1530*. Edited, and with a foreword by Karin Bornkamm. Translated by E. Theodore Bachmann. Philadelphia: Fortress, 1983.

5. Rupp, E. Gordon. *Luther's Progress to the Diet of Worms, 1521*. London: SCM, 1951.

6. Isaac, Gordon L. *Prayer, Meditation & Spiritual Trial: Luther's Account of Life in the Spirit*. Peabody, MA: Hendrickson, 2017.

7. Burnett, Amy Nelson. *Karlstadt and the Origins of the Eucharistic Controversy: A Study in the Circulation of Ideas*. Oxford Studies in Historical Theology. New York: Oxford University Press, 2011.

Chapter 6

1525, a Year of Crisis

As if the world were not topsy-turvy enough already, the closing months of 1524 brought hints of threats of new problems for the Wittenberg team. Imperial determination to eliminate the Lutheran plague that was unsettling the empire had not diminished; at a diet held in Nuremberg in early 1524 the Edict of Worms, mandating eradication of the Lutheran heresy, was renewed. Much more threatened peace and order in the Empire, however. In the summer peasant revolts had broken out in several areas. The fact that some 150 such rebellions had troubled areas throughout much of the German Empire since 1500 did not lessen the anxiety that general disorder from below could threaten the "peace of the land." Political authorities and the general populace longed for that peace, and the authorities sought to establish it through a variety of means.

Other things were troubling the Wittenberg theologians as well. Frederick the Wise died in May 1525; his brother Johann openly supported Luther's and Melanchthon's reforms, so Frederick's death paved the way for more open governmental participation in reforms. They were only slowly beginning to recognize that the state of parish life in the countryside could not be improved through only a few years of preaching. Much more serious at this point, Erasmus announced his decisive break with Luther in his *Diatribe on the Freedom of the Will*, published in September 1524. Among the least of Luther's worries was how to marry off the last of twelve nuns whom a Torgau merchant, Leonhard Koppe, had smuggled out of the Cistercian cloister at Nimbschen. He had brought them to Wittenberg in the spring of 1523, and by the end of 1524 most had found husbands or employment as schoolteachers. The last one radically altered Luther's own life.

Amid these unsettling events, teaching provided a regular routine. By 1525 Luther had returned to the lecture hall. Melanchthon had spurred Luther's own inclination toward reforming the theology curriculum and providing students with the tools they needed for the proper interpretation of Scripture while excising Peter Lombard's textbook on scholastic theology from the curriculum. Although the professors did not embrace a strict division of labor within their teaching of the Scriptures, Melanchthon concentrated more on the New Testament, as did Justus Jonas. Johannes Bugenhagen treated the psalms and Jeremiah as well as a variety of New Testament books. In 1525 Luther began with the Minor Prophets. Later he turned to an occasional lecture course on a New Testament epistle (1 Timothy, Galatians). He concluded his teaching career with treatments of selected psalms and, during his ten-year marathon through Genesis (1535–1545), parts of Isaiah.

Luther was somewhat diverted from his teaching as peasant violence mounted in 1525. Luther had sympathy for some peasant demands. He, as they, opposed the advance of Roman law and the suppression of the Germanic common law that had governed life in Möhra and Mansfeld for centuries. Peasants objected because Roman law's lack of provision for common property deprived the villagers of their traditional control over meadows, fishing streams, forests, and other lands. Nobles were taking these lands into their own domains and wresting the rights to use them from village management. In Saxony noble subjugation of the peasantry was not as severe as in lands to the south and east. Nonetheless, protests against injustice at the hands of those whom Luther believed to be entrusted by God with the care and support of their subjects were quite justified, Luther believed. But the peasants were not to resort to violence. He sometimes condemned peasant pricing of their product in the marketplace and their refusal to pay their pastors or provide for the education of their children. However, he was as critical or even harsher in his denunciation of noble exploitation of those subject to them.

Nonetheless, in the spring of 1525, his *Admonition to Peace, a Reply to the Twelve Articles of the Swabian Peasants* rejected the use of Bible passages for matters that he regarded as secular. Such issues were to be resolved through rational wisdom and a sense of justice. The *Admonition* did reprove princely and noble injustice and exploitation of subjects. However, Luther's chief concern accentuated the need for the preservation of the "peace of the land," the societal order that permitted all to live in safety.

The *Twelve Articles* composed by Christoph Schappler for peasants around Memmingen in early 1525 nominated Luther as a judge of their cause whom they would respect. This document had been adopted by many other local peasant groups. By naming him as a preferred mediator between peasants and princes, Schappler's document placed Luther squarely in the middle of the problem. This was true despite the fact that the peasant program depended on traditional views arising from German common law and also on the writings of others, including the German translation of Erasmus's *Institutes of the Christian Prince* by Zurich pastor Leo Jud, published in 1524.

Reports of peasant disruption and violence, including the murder of noble families, moved Luther to intervene. He recognized his own standing among the peasants, or misestimated it, and ventured into the Thuringian countryside from which he had originated to calm the revolting spirits. There angry peasants confronted him. He saw in the eyes and voices, in the growls and grimaces, of their leaders, and perhaps also in expressions of bewilderment and anxiety in the faces of their followers, how near to the breakdown of public order things had moved. He sensed that many felt coerced and almost captive to their leaders.

His estimate of the peasantry did not improve when he recognized that a former Wittenberg student, Thomas Müntzer, was leading some peasant forces in the region. Müntzer had placed himself in Luther's train, but his spirituality was not content to rest with justification by faith and dependence on external forms of God's Word. He embraced ever more strongly a mystical approach to God that turned to inner feelings rather than to Scripture, the proclamation of its message, and the conveying of the gospel's promise through the sacraments. Luther viewed Müntzer's call for that kind of reform with dread and disgust, for he had come to rely on the solid foundation of the external forms of God's address to sinners rather than his own volatile, fickle feelings.

Therefore, Luther turned his voice against the peasant bands. His *Against the Robbing, Murderous Hordes of Peasant Bands* called for swift execution of punishment on the rebels and the restoration of the "peace of the land" through the use of military might. Negotiations and halfway measures would no longer suffice. His treatise appeared soon

1525, a Year of Crisis

after the forces of the Roman Catholic Duke Georg of Saxony and the Evangelical Landgrave Philip of Hesse had inflicted a severe defeat on the Thuringian peasantry under Müntzer's leadership.[1] Some five thousand died in the battle of Frankenhausen on May 15, 1525. Müntzer was captured fleeing the battlefield and was executed.

Luther issued his own unrepentant defense of his call for suppression of the disturbers of the public peace. At least seven of his followers also came to his defense in print, although some, like Johannes Brenz, called for rulers to exhibit mercy toward the peasants. Luther himself continued to rebuke peasants for high prices in the market and, more frequently, to condemn courtiers and princes for exploitation of their subjects. Contemporary Roman Catholics and many modern scholars have claimed that the revolt of 1525 marked the end of Luther's popularity among the common people, but this is not the case. Preaching and catechetical instruction over the next fifty years did not eliminate public displays of impiety that made the record books of ecclesiastical officials visiting the peasant villages. But the proclamation and teaching of Luther's message shaped the mentality of peasants and patricians over the next century and a half as much as any Christian preaching has ever done.

In the midst of the peasantry's rebellion, Frederick the Wise died, after receiving the Lord's Supper in both kinds. Luther preached two funeral sermons for Frederick; they were published and helped generate the genre of the printed funeral sermon as a memorial and a devotional tool for later generations of Lutherans. Disconcerting as the death

1. The word "evangelical" describes a general orientation to the gospel, and specifically the gospel orientation in Wittenberg. "Evangelical" also describes a group or party in German-speaking lands in the sixteenth century. Finally, the term "Protestant" describes the political identification of Evangelical princes and towns, and the word came into usage after the Speyer "Protestation" of 1529.

of a most influential prince might have been, his brother Johann had much more openly supported Luther's reforms than had the elder sibling. Johann espoused Luther's measures for improving public teaching and practice. The two had become acquainted and then confidants in the decade before Johann assumed the Saxon electorate.

Disconcerting as well must have been the announcement from the last of the escaped nuns of Nimbschen, Katharina von Bora, that she intended to marry either Nikolaus von Amsdorf or Luther himself. The love of her life, a student from a patrician family in Nuremberg, Hieronymus Baumgartner, did not return to Wittenberg after informing his parents on a trip home that he wanted to marry an impoverished noble former nun. Patricians knew that nobility meant little when a bride had abandoned the cloister and was burdened by failed administration of family lands. Luther's candidate for von Bora, Caspar Glatz, the struggling pastor in Orlamünde, Karlstadt's successor there, appealed to Katharina not in the least. Luther suddenly found himself a bridegroom, reluctantly—due to his belief that a man condemned by pope and emperor made less than an ideal possibility for marriage.

The marriage came to be, in Luther's own estimation, one of his greatest blessings from God. Katharina took charge of his rather disorganized personal life. His generosity, which brought him tremendous debts, coupled with his inability to plan his own use of money, was met by her business savvy. She built a small agricultural empire around the Black Cloister, (property at the village of Sülsdorf that her family had lost but that she managed to repurchase) and other assets that she acquired for the family. The elector placed the Black Cloister in the possession of the newly married couple since Luther had been the last resident left living there. Under Katharina's management, their home became a haven for the orphaned children of Luther's two sisters and other relatives, for boarding students and exiled pastors with their families, and even for the Duchess Elisabeth of Denmark, electress of Brandenburg. Her husband, Joachim, drove her to flight because of her commitment to Luther's reform. Luther himself ministered to Elisabeth as she suffered from melancholy as well as an array of physical afflictions over the thirteen years she spent at the Black Cloister. Katharina's aunt Magdalena lived with them and helped administer the servants and service that kept the household running as smoothly as a community of up to several dozen people can.

Katharina also provided Luther with spiritual care. Her even disposition calmed his anxieties and lifted him from his bouts of melancholy as she spoke the gospel of Christ clearly to him. She conveyed this faith to their children as well. Hans was born in 1526; he studied law and served in the Saxon government. Elisabeth's death in 1528, eight months after birth, broke the hearts of her parents, who grieved even as they were confident that God's baptismal promise had carried her to his throne. Magdalena was born in 1529. The noblewoman Argula von Grumbach, an active supporter of Luther's reforms, gave the father counsel on how his wife should wean the baby when she visited Luther at the Coburg castle in 1530. Next came Martin, born 1531; then Paul, born 1533; and Margarethe, born 1534. Martin studied theology but never became a pastor; alcohol took his life at age thirty-four. Paul studied medicine at Melanchthon's urging. His command of health science and other studies of nature earned him a professorship at the University of Jena and appointment as personal court physician to several princes, including Electors Joachim II of Brandenburg and August of Saxony.

Luther's expressions of grief when Magdalena died at age thirteen reveal his deep love for his children. Particularly Hans may have suffered under strict parental discipline, but the relationships with his children that Luther reported reflect his love and his appreciation of their ability to teach him the gospel. After Hans's birth, his references to God as father and his people as the children of their Maker increased. Family life provided perhaps his favorite analogies for the relationship between Creator and human creatures.

At year's end 1525, Luther finally, reluctantly, took up the challenge issued more than twelve months earlier by Erasmus to the very heart of his theology, as he said: his recognition that his will was bound to make false choices when it sought to find God. Early on, Luther had recognized that his will was inevitably bound to make false choices when it sought to find refuge from threats, to seek an ultimate source of all good. (In his Large Catechism Luther described God as a refuge from all that threatens and as the source of all good.) As a young man, at home and in the cloister, Luther had tried to force his will to love God. The harder he tried, the more he realized that his will did not really like God since his efforts to please his Creator were, Luther honestly admitted, always less than perfect. Peace came to his troubled spirit only when his Ockhamist convictions regarding God's almighty power propelled him to view God as the one who loves his chosen people without any condition on their part. God must re-create sinners into his children, just as children are born without their parents' gaining their consent. Only through a realization of their dependence on God's creating love for their existence could believers focus first on God and then on their neighbors' needs. Otherwise, they would continually try to manipulate God with sacred activities and would turn other human beings into instruments of their own efforts to win God's favor. Luther expressed this belief in his *On Bound Choice* [*De servo arbitrio*], which came from the press of Hans Lufft, one of his favorite Wittenberg printers, at the end of December 1525. It commanded an instant readership and won the hearts of many young humanists. They still wanted to profit from Erasmus's scholarship but found Luther's proclamation of the biblical message convincing and consoling. That comforting message included the boundness of human choice when deciding between God and idols, for if the decision rested on God and not themselves, then Luther (and his readers) would have to rely on the promise God had made in Jesus Christ alone. After 1526 this work fell into obscurity.

But Luther did not fall into obscurity. Still certain that he was working within the structures of the papal church, he worked ever harder for its reform and turned to a series of measures to implement reform at the parish level.

INTERVIEWS

Pastor Mathesius, can you shed some light on Luther's criticism of the peasants in the revolt of 1525? In the fall of 1524 the peasants around Lake Constance rose up in arms, but this mischief was pacified. In the next year there was a brutal uprising of the peasants in Swabia, Lorraine, and Franconia, for whom a rebellious Doctor [in fact, a furrier, Christoph Schappeler] composed twelve articles. Doctor Luther responded to them on the basis of good argumentation from God's Word, and he warned people who were being deceived of the harm. For there has never been a rebel who forgot his oath and duty to his government that profited from rebellion. God has confirmed governmental authority and obedient submission to it with the words of his Son [Matt 22:21] and commanded all to be obedient with all that they have to the authorities established by God's ordering for the sake of conscience and because of punishment [Rom 13:5]. Luther admonished the ruling authorities not to misunderstand God's Word but to submit to its discipline, as King David preached in Psalm 2, that they deal reasonably with kindness and mercy with those who were being led astray (so that God in his wrath would not destroy them and devour them as he does tyrants). For there is no judge on earth so important that he does not have to answer to one above him. But the peasants stopped up their ears and in bloodthirsty, devilish fashion pursued their course under the name and cover of the gospel. They attacked not only monasteries and clergy but also their own rulers, stabbed a count through with a spear, and burned and razed the castles of nobles. This caused Doctor Luther to defend God's order and the duties of the authorities. With a very harsh book he condemned the arrogant, bloodthirsty undertaking of the peasants and admonished those rulers that were paralyzed with fear that they should and could rein in and reduce such harmful passions with the power of the sword. Doctor Luther was severely criticized by the peasants and their spokesmen and rebellious preachers, and many others were displeased with his severity and harshness. But Doctor Luther offered good, sound reasons for what had driven him to writing so rashly and sharply. He told how the results and subsequent experiences of such situations gave proof and support that for such a situation, books of this kind were necessary. For they had forgotten their oaths and duties, and they had attacked their rulers, doing nothing but stealing and robbing, and they wanted to cover and excuse their godless arrogance with the gospel. God saw what was right and supported his vice regents, so that the Swabian League pacified the uprising in Swabia, Franconia, and around Salzburg. Many fell to God's

1525, a Year of Crisis

vengeance. Many reasonable lords pacified their erring subjects in a gentle and moderate fashion.[2]

Doctor Luther, your stance against the peasants in 1525 has gotten criticism from the very beginning. What was your thinking in opposing the peasant armies? Suppose I were to break into a man's house, rape his wife and daughters, break open his safe and take his money, put his sword to his chest, and say, "if you will not put up with this, I shall run you through, for you are a godless wretch." Then if a crowd gathered and were about to kill me, or if the judge ordered my head cut off, suppose I were to cry out, "Hey, Christ teaches you to be merciful and not to kill me," what would people say? That is exactly what these peasants and their sympathizers are now doing. Now that they have, like robbers, murderers, thieves, and scoundrels, done what they pleased to their masters, they want to put on a song and dance about mercy . . . Here you see the intention of those who condemn my book as though it forbade mercy. It is certain that they are either peasants, rebels, and bloodhounds themselves or have been misled by such people, for they would like all wickedness to go unpunished. Thus, under the name of mercy they would be—so far as it is in their power—the most merciless and cruel destroyers of the whole world . . . There are two realms, one God's realm, the other the realm of this world . . . God's realm is a realm of grace and mercy, not of wrath and punishment. In it there is only forgiveness, consideration for one another, love, service, the doing of good, peace, joy, etc. But the realm of the world is a realm of wrath and severity. In it there is only punishment, repression, judgment, and condemnation to restrain the wicked and protect the good . . . The Scripture passages that speak of mercy apply to God's realm and to Christians, not to the realm of the world, for it is

2. Mathesius, *Historien*, XLVIa.

a Christian's obligation not only to be merciful but also to endure every kind of suffering . . . The realm of this world should not be merciful but strict and severe in expressing God's wrath against sin in fulfilling its work and duty . . . It is turned only against the wicked to hold them in check and keep them at peace and to protect and save the righteous [Rom 13:3–4] . . . Although the severity and wrath of the world's kingdom seems unmerciful, nevertheless, when we see it rightly, it is not the least of God's mercies. Let everyone consider and decide the following case. Suppose I had a wife and children, a house, servants and property, and a thief or murderer fell upon me, killed me in my own house, ravished my wife and children, took all that I had and went unpunished, so that he could do the same thing again wherever he wished. Tell me, who would be more in need of mercy in such a case, I or the thief and murderer?[3]

Doctor Luther, you began quite early to use the work of Erasmus, yet is it true that you were never quite comfortable with him? In 1517 already, I wrote to my friend Johann Lang, "I am reading our Erasmus, but daily I dislike him more and more. Nevertheless, it pleases me that he is constantly and learnedly exposing and condemning the monks and priests for their deep-rooted and lame ignorance. I am afraid, however, that he does not promote the cause of Christ and the grace of God sufficiently . . . Human things have a greater weight with him than the divine. Although I pass judgment upon him reluctantly, nevertheless I do it to warn you not to read everything, or rather, not to accept everything without scrutiny. We live in perilous times. I see that not everyone is a truly wise Christian just because he knows Greek and Hebrew."[4] Four years later I wrote to Georg Spalatin, "I see that Erasmus is far from the knowl-

3. WA 18:388–91; LW 46:68–71.
4. WA Br 1:90; LW 48:40, Nr. 36.

1525, a Year of Crisis

edge of grace since in all his writings he is not concerned about the cross but wants peace. He thinks that everything should be discussed and treated in a polite manner and with a certain benevolent kindliness. But Behemoth [Luther followed Jerome in interpreting the beast in Job 40:15–24, as the devil] pays no attention, and we gain nothing by that approach. As I read in his preface to the New Testament, I mused that he must have been thinking of himself when he wrote, 'The Christian easily despises glory.' I thought, 'Erasmus, I am afraid you deceive yourself.' It is a great thing to despise glory. But his way of despising glory was to think lightly of it, not to bear the contempt that others put upon him. Despising glory is really nothing if it is only put into words; it is even less than nothing if you are only thinking it."[5]

You waited over a year to reply to Erasmus's "Diatribe on the Freedom of the Will" after he published it in the autumn of 1524. Why did you decide finally to take up his challenge to conduct a disputation on the subject? At the beginning of my work on the boundness of the will's ability to choose to turn itself toward God, I wrote, "I confess not only that you are far superior to me in powers of eloquence and native genius (which we all must admit, all the more as I am an uncultivated fellow who has always moved in uncultivated circles), but you have quite dampened my spirit and my enthusiasm and left me exhausted before I could strike a blow. There are two reasons for this: first, your cleverness in treating the subject with such remarkable and consistent moderation as to make it impossible for me to be angry with you, and second, the fortune or chance or fate by which you say nothing on this important subject that has not been said before."[6] But I also had to tell him that I found it "intolerable that

5. WA Br 2:387; LW 48:306, Nr. 429.
6. WA 18:600–601; LW 33:15–16.

113

you count this subject of free choice among the things that are useless and unnecessary and replace it with a list of the things you consider sufficient for the Christian religion. It is the kind of list that any Jew or heathen totally ignorant of Christ could certainly draw up with ease, for you make not the slightest mention of Christ, as if you think that Christian godliness can exist without Christ, so long as God is worshipped as being by nature most merciful with all the power a person commands.[7]

But in fact, you invested a lot in writing one of your longest books to refute him, and your argumentation convinced and won the allegiance of many who had admired you both. Finally, I too, had to admit that the question of the will's freedom drove me to despair, but as I wrote to Erasmus, "Let us take it that there are three lights—the light of nature, the light of grace, and the light of glory, to use the common, valid distinction. By the light of nature it is an insoluble problem how it can be just that a good person should suffer and a bad person prosper, but this problem is solved by the light of grace. By the light of grace it is an insoluble problem how God can damn a person who is unable by any power of his own to do anything but sin and be guilty. Here both the light of nature and the light of grace tell us that it is not the fault of the wretched person but of an unjust god. For they cannot judge otherwise of a god who crowns one ungodly person freely and apart from personal merits, yet condemns another who may well be less, or at least not more, ungodly. But the light of glory tells us differently, and it will show us hereafter that the god whose judgment here is one of incomprehensible righteousness is a God of most perfect and obvious righteousness. In the meantime, we can only believe this, being admonished and confirmed by the example of the light of grace. It performs a similar miracle in

7. WA 18:609; LW 33:29.

1525, a Year of Crisis

relation to the light of nature."[8] So at the end, I summarized what I wrote in these words, "If we believe that Christ has redeemed human beings by his blood, we are bound to confess that the whole person was lost. Otherwise, we would make Christ either superfluous or the redeemer of only the lowest part of the human being. That would be blasphemy and sacrilege." But I also expressed my thanks: "I praise and commend you highly for this, that unlike all the others, you alone have addressed the real issue, the essence of the matter in dispute, and have not wearied me with irrelevancies about the papacy, purgatory, indulgences, and such similar trifles (for they are trifles rather than basic issues) . . . You and you alone have seen the question on which everything hinges and have aimed at the vital spot. For this I sincerely thank you."[9]

Doctor Luther, why did you decide to marry? I did it to silence the evil mouths that are so used to complaining about me. For I still hope to live for a little while. In addition, I also did not want to reject this unique opportunity to obey my father's wish for children, which he so often expressed. At the same time, I also wanted to confirm what I have taught by practicing it. For I find so many timid people in spite of such great light from the gospel. God has willed and brought about this step. For I feel neither passionate love nor a burning desire for my spouse, but I cherish her.[10]

Your wife took over management of the household, did she not? My lord Käthe drives the wagon, takes care of the fields, buys cattle and manages them in the pasture, brews beer, and other things. In between, she has started to read the Bible, and I have promised her fifty gulden if she

8. WA 18:785; LW 33:292.
9. WA 18:786; LW 33:293–94.
10. WA Br 3:541; LW 49:117, Nr. 900.

finishes before Easter. She is going at it very seriously and is now starting the Book of Deuteronomy.[11]

Tell us more about her. I would not trade my Käthe for Frankfurt or Venice, first because God gave her to me, and second, because I often notice that she is much better than other women although she has her failings, too. But she has so many greater virtues. Third she is a true and faithful wife. All that overcomes the disagreement and discord that Satan likes to cultivate between married people.[12] . . . The greatest grace and gift of God is having a pious, kind, God-fearing spouse who maintains the household well, with whom you can live in peace, to whom you can entrust all that you own and possess, even your very body and life, with whom you can raise your children. God imposes so many things upon a marriage that the husband and wife have not planned. Käthe has a pious husband, who loves her, and she is an empress. I am so thankful to God for her. But for this part of life it is necessary to have a pious and God-fearing person.[13]

Doctor Luther, you once tried to induce your son Hans to behave while you were away from Wittenberg. What did you write to him? I simply wrote, "my dear son, I am happy to learn that you are doing well in school and that you are praying diligently. Continue to do so, and when I return home, I shall bring you a nice present from the fair. I know of a beautiful, nice, delightful garden where are many children wearing little golden coats. They pick up delicious apples, pears, cherries, and yellow and blue plums under the trees. They are singing, jumping, and having fun. They also have nice ponies with golden reins and silver saddles. I asked the owner of the garden whose children they were. He told me, 'These are the children who like to pray, study,

11. WA Br 7:316–17; LW 50:108–9, Nr. 2267.

12. WA TR 1:17, Nr. 49.

13. WA TR 2:497, Nr. 2506.

and behave.' Then I said, 'Dear sir, I also have a son, whose name is Hänschen Luther. Might he not also be permitted to enter the garden, so that he could feast on such good apples and pears and ride on these pretty ponies and play with these children?' The man replied, 'If he too likes to pray, study, and behave, he too may enter the garden and also his friends Phil [the son of Melanchthon] and Justie [the son of Justus Jonas]. When they are all together, they will also get whistles, drums, lutes, and all kinds of instruments, and they will also be able to dance and shoot little crossbows.' ... Therefore, dear Hänschen, do study and pray hard, and tell Phil and Justie to study and pray, too. Then you all will get into the garden together. With this, I commend you to the protection of the dear Lord."[14]

Doctor Luther, you loved your children and mourned over the deaths, first of your infant daughter Elisabeth, and then of Magdalena, who died at age thirteen. As she lay severely ill, I asked her, "Sweet Magdalena, my little daughter, would you rather stay with me, your father, or go to your other father?" Magdalena answered, "As God wills," and I said, "You dear sweet daughter. The spirit is strong, but the flesh is weak." I turned away and said, "I love her so very much. The flesh is so strong, what is going to happen with the spirit? God has given no bishop in a thousand years as great a gift as he has given me, and a person must boast of such gifts. I am angry with myself that I cannot rejoice or be thankful for this gift at this point although I will come to the time when I can sing God a song and thank him a bit for this gift." And when she died, I had to say, "I want to hang on to my daughter, for I love her very much. But if it is your will, dear God, that you take her, I will gladly know that she is with you." Philip was with me at the time and commented, "Parental love is a metaphor; it is the image

14. WA Br 5:377-78, Nr. 1595; LW 49:323-24.

of the Godhead, which is impressed into the human race. How great the love of parents for their children is! It is as Scripture says truly huge and passionate."[15]

You and your wife composed two epitaphs for her, one cast in her own words. What did you say in the first, and what did you have her saying in the second?

First,

> Magdalena, Luther's child so dear,
> Is finding rest among the saints, not here,
> And now her bed is planted in the earth,
> For none of us attains a better berth.
> A daughter's born to live and then to die.
> Because of sin no other way goes by
> That death that Christ's blood turns to life
> And blesses us with peace beyond all strife.

And then, with Katharina, we wrote:

> I, Lena, Luther's dear, dear child,
> Am sleeping now with all saints mild
> And lie in my own peace and rest
> For now I am our God's own guest.
> A mortal child I was indeed
> Was born of mother's mortal seed,
> But now I live so rich in God
> Because of Christ's dear death and blood.[16]

DISCUSSION QUESTIONS

1. Why did Luther react to the situation of the peasants in 1525 the way he did?

15. WA TR 5:190, Nr. 5494.
16. WA, TR 5:186,19–26, Nr. 5490c.

2. How do Luther's opinions and concerns in regard to civic disorder for a just cause compare to those of U.S. citizens today?
3. What were the points of difference that divided Erasmus and Luther, and why were they important to each of them?
4. Imagine an evening in the Black Cloister with Martin and Katherine and their family and guests.
5. What moved a sixteenth-century person like Martin Luther to react to death the way he did?

FURTHER READING

1. The biographies and overviews of Luther's theology listed in the introduction.
2. Bornkamm, Heinrich. *Luther in Mid-Career, 1521–1530*. Edited, and with a foreword by Karin Bornkamm. Translated by E. Theodore Bachmann. Philadelphia: Fortress, 1983.
3. Kolb, Robert. *Bound Choice, Election, and Wittenberg Theological Method: From Martin Luther to the Formula of Concord*. Lutheran Quarterly Books. Grand Rapids: Eerdmans, 2005.
4. Lazareth, William H. *Luther on the Christian Home: An Application of the Social Ethics of the Reformation*. Philadelphia: Muhlenberg, 1960.
5. DeRusha, Michelle. *Katharina and Martin Luther: The Radical Marriage of a Runaway Nun and a Renegade Monk*. Grand Rapids: Baker, 2017.

6. Karant-Nunn, Susan C., and Merry E. Wiesner-Hanks, eds. and trans. *Luther on Women: A Sourcebook*. Cambridge: Cambridge University Press, 2003.

Chapter 7

The Institutionalization of the Movement

REFORM MEANS MORE THAN changing one element or a few elements of an institution and a way of life. Luther's new definitions of the basic terminology that stands at the core of the Christian faith and its practice sent ripples through church and society. In the years immediately following 1526, Luther did not realize that a new church was forming around him. He did recognize that practical transformations of many aspects of life would flow from his redefinition of what it means to be Christian. For it led to a shift of the Christian's focus from approaching God with sacred activities, devoted to pleasing him and winning his favor, to receiving God's gifts that come through his speaking to sinners in Christ.

Luther's composition of model sermons in his postil, begun at the Wartburg in 1522, was carried on in the late 1520s by a former student, Stephen Roth. Roth had returned from his study in Wittenberg to his native Zwickau to serve as school rector and then town secretary or administrator. His editorial work did not always meet Luther's expectations or approval. Roth not only prepared model sermons from the notes he had taken as he listened to Luther preach during four years of study in Wittenberg. He also added sermons, to round out the full complement for each Sunday from his own theological imagination, which did not match the quality of Luther's thinking. But Luther was at least somewhat grateful for the provision of this helpful tool for parish preachers.

Luther asserted in 1526 that the preaching and teaching of God's Word are "the most important part of the divine service."[1] He realized the importance of the liturgy. It helped worshipers express their praise and prayer, it was the setting for proclaiming and receiving God's Word, and it was the vehicle that formed faith and piety. But the proclaimed Word of God informed the entire Christian life. In 1523 Luther had excised the canon of the mass from the liturgy. The canon contained the words regarded as a repetition of Christ's sacrifice for sin on Calvary's cross. Thus, in the popular mind, the canon delivered forgiveness to the participants. Luther's revised form for worship retained Latin as its language, but he was making available German forms for baptism and confession and absolution as well as for marriage ceremonies. In 1526 he issued his *German Mass*, a simplified liturgy that employed hymns for the several parts of the traditional liturgy. Most congregations and territories that were introducing his reforms adhered more closely to the traditional forms and texts but in German translation. Slowly congregations made more and more use of the hymnals that Luther had prepared or overseen. For them he himself prepared over two dozen hymns that conveyed his understanding of the biblical message.

Luther's emphasis on preaching changed other rites as well. Medieval funerals had to take place within twenty-four

1. WA 19:78, 26–27; LW 53:68.

to thirty-six hours of death for sanitary reasons. The priest did not necessarily accompany the corpse to the grave. Instead, the sexton gathered with the relatives and neighbors at the home, escorting casket and family to the cemetery, singing dirges, with the boys' school choir leading them. The sexton read Scripture and said prayers. The chief ritual for the dead came with the subsequent mass for the deceased's relief in purgatory—for most, the first of many such masses. Quickly, Luther's adherents introduced the singing of hymns of resurrection and consolation, and gradually a sermon became an integral part of burial. Wedding ceremonies also took on a more religious character and came to include a sermon. Luther's example of preaching at a few weddings for students and other friends modeled such sermons. Burial and marriage sermons found their way into print as devotional literature in the years following Luther's death.

The mid-1520s saw much more rapid and widespread deviation from some of Luther's central concerns related to the proper teaching of the biblical message and the pastoral care of Christ's people. Andreas Karlstadt set Luther's teeth on edge with his denial of the presence of Christ's body and blood in the Lord's Supper and his rejection of infant baptism and baptismal regeneration. Luther felt betrayed by a confidant who had shared his views earlier. Karlstadt's public disagreement, expressed in several brief treatises in 1524 and a flood of subsequent supplementary pamphlets, led to more controversy.

Ulrich Zwingli had enthusiastically acclaimed Luther as the third Elijah, the long-awaited prophet of the end times, in 1519. But his horror at the superstitious use of material objects for manipulating spiritual and temporal blessings, and his grounding in the Realist philosophy of the medieval school labeled the *via antiqua* (old way), prevented him from accepting Luther's insistence on the literal interpretation of Christ's words in instituting the Lord's Supper: "this is my body," and "this is my blood." Luther's Ockhamist background made it easy for him to believe that God could select objects of his created order, including human language and sacramental elements, to serve as instruments that actually accomplished his will to forgive sins and grant salvation. Luther's belief in the unlimited power of the Almighty Creator made it impossible for him to understand why a believer could not accept that God could make even the body and blood of his incarnate Son present with bread and wine to convey the promise comprehended in the words of the institution of the Lord's Supper.

Another active supporter of Wittenberg reform, Johannes Oecolampadius, who had settled into a leadership role in introducing reform in Basel, joined Zwingli in attacking Luther's belief in the true presence of Christ's body and blood in the Lord's Supper. A series of treatises brought the conflict to the wider public in the years between 1525 and 1529. Johannes Brenz and others came to Luther's side; others expressed their support for Oecolampadius and Zwingli. In 1527 and 1528 Luther composed two longer treatises presenting his teaching on the presence of Christ and the power of the promise given in the Lord's Supper: *That the Words, "This is my Body," etc. Still Stand*; and *Confession on the Lord's Supper*. They continued to guide Lutheran teaching long after the reformer's death.

Zwingli and Oecolampadius insisted on the baptism of infants as the sign of their entry into the Christian community. By 1525, however, others, including fellow residents of Zwingli's Zurich, began to advocate publicly a believer's baptism. They rejected Luther's view that the promise of forgiveness articulated in baptism conveys that forgiveness to infants. Zwingli sharply opposed Anabaptists in Zurich,

The Institutionalization of the Movement

where executions of those who rejected infant baptism began in 1525. By 1528 Luther was contending with a few Anabaptist preachers in Saxony as well.

Although most Anabaptists insisted on Christian abstinence from any role in secular government, one group of Dutch Anabaptists gathered in exile in the town of Münster and gradually took over rule in the town in 1534. Münster was under the governance of the bishop, Franz von Waldeck. The leaders of the immigrants from the Netherlands, Jan Mathijs and Jan van Leiden, introduced polygamy and the sharing of goods. This concept of communal property largely served to disenfranchise, dispossess, and then exile some two thousand members of Münster's middle class to the advantage of the exiles from elsewhere. Mathijs died in battle trying to spread the kingdom. Van Leiden claimed to be a new King David. The military forays of the members of van Leiden's royal forces provoked an alliance of Landgrave Philip of Hesse with Habsburg forces from the Netherlands and Bishop Franz. The kingdom was brought to an end through siege on June 25, 1535, and through the subsequent executions of its leaders. This placed the town firmly under episcopal control. Luther aided the propaganda campaign against this kingdom and its theology. For more than a century both Evangelicals and Roman Catholics used Münster to associate all Anabaptists, most of whom were pacifists, with violence and rebellion.

Closer to home, Luther's and Melanchthon's former student Johann Agricola, school rector in Eisleben, may have not understood why in 1526 the elector chose to give Melanchthon a second professorship, adding one in theology to his position as teacher of Greek in the arts faculty. Agricola expected that he himself would be called back to Wittenberg. That does not explain why Agricola developed his insistence that God's law does not have anything to say to believers in Christ, but it may explain his sharp attacks on Melanchthon in 1527 and 1528. Agricola's views on the law of God in the Christian life had already been expressed in some of his writing. He had learned from Luther that the law accuses and condemns sin and sinners, but he had not captured Luther's understanding of the Christian life as a struggle between faith and doubt, obedience and sin. Thus, he taught that the gospel of Christ is the only message that applies to Christians. God's law governs civic life but has no role for believers. Agricola did not deny that faith produces new obedience to God, but he believed that the call to repentance and instructions for daily Christian living should be labeled "gospel." Melanchthon recognized that this destroyed the proper distinction of law and gospel, so necessary for the proper application of the biblical message to Christian lives. Agricola's attack on Melanchthon evoked the concern of Elector Johann. He arranged for conversation between the two in 1528, with Luther taking a mediating role. The dispute was not so much resolved as delayed for a decade when Agricola gave ground to Luther's reinforcement of Melanchthon's arguments.

Elector Johann had concern for the parish life of his domains. Soon after his brother's death he urged his Wittenberg theologians to revive the medieval custom of visitation of local congregations. He mandated that this visitation be conducted no longer under the auspices of the bishops, who remained loyal to the pope and to medieval practices, but under princely sponsorship. Throughout the fifteenth century German princes had followed the example of French and English rulers in assuming more and more responsibility for the spiritual welfare and church life in their lands. After some false starts, Melanchthon, with Luther's aid, drafted regulations for the visitors, and thus for congregational life. The "Saxon Visitation Articles" of

1528 were not the first attempt at formulating a framework for parish life in an Evangelical territory. Philip, Landgrave of Hesse, had called a synod in the town of Homburg in 1526; there his ecclesiastical advisors drew up rules for the conduct of priests and parishioners. Luther found them too burdensome and advised against their adoption. Landgrave Philip introduced many of the measures in these "Homburg Articles" nonetheless.

The "Saxon Visitation Articles" contained cues for good preaching and provisions for liturgical forms and practice, for the conduct and use of the sacraments, for care for the poor and sick, for schooling (including detailed plans for the curriculum of individual grade levels), and for church leadership on the electorate level. Given Agricola's denial of a use for the law in the Christian life, the "Visitation Articles'" paid careful attention to the application of the distinction of law and gospel, with treatments of the freedom of the will and Christian freedom that emphasized new obedience and the discipline of daily repentance.

The "Saxon Visitation Articles" provided a springboard for other territories and municipalities to draft directives for the conduct of worship, social welfare provisions, and education in villages and towns. Several prominent followers of Luther gave counsel and guidance for composing such church ordinances. Wittenberg pastor and professor Johannes Bugenhagen left his colleagues repeatedly in the late 1520s and in subsequent decades in order to assist towns, principalities, and even the kingdom of Denmark in drawing up such regulations for ecclesiastical life. In the southern German lands Johannes Brenz, pastor in Schwäbisch Hall, and Andreas Osiander, pastor in Nuremberg, constructed church ordinances for use in Nuremberg and the nearby principality of Brandenburg-Ansbach in

1533. These ordinances served as models for a number of governments that chose to introduce Luther's reforms.

The visitation of parishes in which Luther and Melanchthon participated impressed them both with the sad state of village spiritual life. Thus, Luther took upon himself an assignment he had been trying to impose on colleagues—the task of preparing a manual for Christian instruction. "Catechism" was the name for the traditional program of instruction of the medieval church. Its core elements accentuated faith (taught through the Apostles' Creed), hope (the Lord's Prayer), and love (originally lists of virtues and vices but the Ten Commandments by the fifteenth century). Printed catechisms had begun to appear for the instruction of children in the late fifteenth century, but in general, sermons conveyed the catechism to most people in the Middle Ages. Most did not go to school and experience classroom instruction. By Luther's time catechetical handbooks (*enchiridia*) had found their way into print in various versions and formats. As an Augustinian, Luther had often preached on the "catechism." He continued the practice in the 1520s. In 1528 and early 1529 he preached his way three times through the Creed, the Lord's Prayer, and the Decalogue as well as through the sacraments of baptism and the Lord's Supper.

While he was preaching the last series of sermons on the Decalogue, the Apostles' Creed, and the Lord's Prayer—the three core items in the medieval catechism—as well as on the sacraments, Luther also began to compose a catechism in three forms: first a wall chart, then an *enchiridion* (a handbook for adults teaching children, which became the Small Catechism), and a longer catechism (called the Large Catechism or German Catechism); this larger catechism included treatments of the three core elements and of the sacraments. Luther's *Prayerbook* had proposed changing the order of the elements of the medieval catechism so that believers could diagnose their sinful state through the Ten Commandments before hearing the cure for that state in the gospel of the Apostles' Creed and acting on it according to the pattern set forth in the Lord's Prayer. He then treated the sacramental forms of God's promise, baptism and the Lord's Supper. In his 1529 *Enchiridion* the reformer turned this overview of Christian teaching into a handbook for Christian living by adding two sections. First, he composed instructions for prayer along with daily meditation on the biblical message by reviewing the Apostles' Creed or the Lord's Prayer. Second, he formulated a "household chart," which sketched his vision of the callings of daily service to others in home and occupation, society and congregation. This represented his application of medieval social theory to the life of every believer.

Important for daily Christian life in Luther's view was the use of God's Word in baptism, the Lord's Supper, and confession and absolution. Objecting to the uncertainty instilled by the medieval opinion that only those mortal sins confessed to the priest could be forgiven, Luther and his colleagues rejected the necessity of enumerating all sins. They cultivated the remorse and sorrow over breaking God's commands and not trusting in him as they emphasized the forgiveness of sins. The power of forgiveness lay in God's promise, and Luther proclaimed the ability of all Christians to speak that word to one another.

During these years distractions—above all the steadily advancing Ottoman armies—diverted Charles V's attention somewhat from the "Lutheran problem" in his German lands. In 1526 he had reminded the assembled princes and municipal governments of the Edict of Worms, instructing them to "carry it out in accordance with their consciences." Evangelical governments interpreted that in their own favor. Thus, in 1529, when the imperial diet met again in Speyer, Charles had his brother and regent for the German Empire, King Ferdinand, make it clear that the eradication of the Lutheran heresy remained imperial policy. Elector Johann's chancellor, Gregor Brück, led the composition of a response in the genre of the imperial *protestatio*: this was more than a "protest"; rather it was a legal brief giving testimony to the justice of a cause, in objection to the emperor's decree. The political leaders of the Evangelical reform movement henceforth bore the label "Protestants."

INTERVIEWS

Brother Hoffmeister, to what do you ascribe the growth of the movement centered in your Augustinian cloister in Wittenberg that you regard as heretical? Will no one have the nerve to say, "Everything was written long ago, so is it necessary to repeat it?" The answer is, the rabble writes nothing new, but they lie and deceive this year just like last. Or is it not just as good to publish the truth as often as they publish lies. But this movement has grown because it is tireless in stuffing its false, deceptive teaching down the throats of the common people. You see how they write so sincerely, in Latin, in German. They translate, they print; there is no end to it. Luther cannot utter a single word when he is dead drunk but that it appears in print immediately. Indeed, it is not just Luther's words and deeds but also the image that he and his nun project. I will not say anything about their visitations and their catechisms. To sum it all up, whatever may serve in one or another form to maintain and support this undertaking will certainly not be neglected, indeed, not put off for a day. What do we do? How do we react? Not at all, but we act as if Christ is our prisoner and must and should do only what we want. Let me emphasize, dear brethren, it is no little worry of mine that Christ will soon say to us, "the kingdom will be taken from you and given its fruit to the Gentiles [Matt. 21:43]."[2]

Pastor Spangenberg, what kind of reception were Luther's writings receiving in these days? When one of his treatises first came off the press in Wittenberg, some copies left off the title page Doctor Luther's name and Wittenberg as the place of publication, and omitted the preface and a few other words. That kind of copy was delivered to Georg of Saxony as a product from some far-off place. When he read the booklet, it hit him just right, and he praised it highly, also to Lucas Cranach the elder, who was working in Dresden at the time. He said, "See, Lucas, you always praise your monk in Wittenberg, Luther, as the only person who is so learned and who speaks and writes German so well. But you are wrong in that as in other things. Look, here I have a little book that is as good or better than anything that Luther could ever make." He drew it from his jacket and scolded the painter. But Lucas looked at it and said, "Gracious prince and lord, Luther did write this book. His name is simply not on it. I have another copy of it, which he gave me, with his name printed on it." The duke looked at it and saw that it was nothing else but by Luther. He got terribly angry and lost his temper, cursing and saying, "It is really a shame that such a hideous monk should write such a good book."[3]

Pastor Spalatin, what happened in 1524 that others who sought reform began to criticize Luther's way of reformation? About this time, as the holy and pure Word of God was being broadcast, it happened, in the words of the proverb, that "where God has placed a church, the devil places a chapel

---

2. Volz, ed., *Drei Schriften*, 117.
3. Spangenberg, *Adel*, 1:8, 3.

next to it." So from time to time new sects have always arisen. That is what happened with the raging and insults against both the sacrament of holy baptism and of the true body and blood of Christ. Doctor Andreas Bodenstein von Karlstadt was the first, and he attacked both sacraments. Thereafter, Zwingli and Oecolampadius and many others at Strassburg, from time to time, fell into this head over heels. They brought almost all of Switzerland into their camp and wanted to make of the sacrament a spiritual eating and drinking. Doctor Martin Luther wrote me as I went to Altenburg that in one single year eight different erring opinions and positions had grown up against the most precious sacrament of the altar. Doctor Balthasar Hubmayer of Friedberg initiated an erring sect that became so strong in Moravia and Silesia that practically the whole of those lands was squandered away, poisoned, and led astray. Finally, in 1528, he was burned at the stake in Vienna. The poorer peasants and their wives entered such groups. So did the dreamers and the spiritualists, who only wanted to act on their own revelations and with the spirit and had only contempt for and rejected God's external, oral Word. They went so far as to reject infant baptism, regarded baptism as nothing more than a handful of water, and even spoke of the baptism of the dog. Some attacked the holy divine Trinity, including Campanus in the Netherlands, Schwenckfeld, and others. Almost all the ancient heresies that had been present in the early church were revived. Finally, through Doctor Martin Luther, Philip Melanchthon, Doctor Pomeranus, and other Christian scholars God acted so graciously that these people wrote and preached against those dangerous, devilish sects and reduced their appeal, and in this way they were properly criticized. For the Anabaptists in Thuringia, Hesse, Moravia, Silesia—especially in Moravia—gained the upper hand. The Anabaptists went beyond that and became rebellious against secular authorities, and finally many of them perished by the sword. Finally, at the peak of this development they did not want to permit the simple, pure, comforting gospel of Christ, just as under the papal kings, princes, bishops, and cities, as it happened in Münster in Westphalia.[4]

Doctor Cochlaeus, how did you appraise Luther's defense of the true presence of Christ's body and blood in the Lord's Supper? When Luther saw that Zwingli and Oecolampadius were growing stronger by the day, he wrote another very long book against them in German, titled *Confession concerning Christ's Supper*. In its first part he censures and refutes Zwingli; in the second, Ocolampadius; and finally, in the third part, he offers the confession of his faith, which he orders to be taken for the certain and final opinion of his mind, both in his lifetime and after his death. In the first part, he brings many reproaches against Zwingli and his accomplices, which the Catholics had earlier, and more correctly, brought against Luther himself. For instance, that disagreement and division of this sort among them come not from the Holy Spirit but from Satan; that their spirit of confusion contradicts itself; that it should easily be concluded that the devil, the father of all dissension, is their teacher; that dissension in the way you think and the way you speak comes from the devil, etc. In the second part Luther contradicts himself when he denies that there was wine at Christ's supper since Christ had said, "I shall not drink of fruit of the vine," etc. [Matt. 26:29]. But he had previously confirmed this point, both in his *Babylonian Captivity* and elsewhere, when he derided transubstantiation and the doctrine of accidents without substance. He also affirms that Christ did not only give the cup to his disciples, but

4. Spalatin, "Annales," 92–94.

drank from it himself as well, which he had denied earlier in his book *On the Abolition of the Mass*. In it he taught that the priests ought to give the sacrament to others but ought not partake of it themselves since this is what Christ did—he gave it to others but did not himself partake. Moreover, in the third part, he lists among the articles of his faith that free will must not be believed. "I here reject and condemn," he says, "as pure errors every doctrine which boasts of our free will. Moreover, I affirm that vigils, masses, and anniversary days for the dead are useless, and anniversary masses are of the devil. And also, that the saints must not be invoked. And also, that extreme unction, matrimony, and the ordination of priests are not sacraments. But above all other abominations I regard the mass, and the foundation chapters, or monasteries of the church as they now are set up, to be the worst, but, God granting it, they will soon lie in ruins. For however great, weighty, and shameful a sinner I have been, who wasted and lost my youth in a damnable manner, nevertheless, these were my greatest sins, that I was so holy a monk, and for more than fifteen years so horribly offended my beloved Lord with so many masses and inflicted martyrdom and tortures on him." These things Luther said in that book![5]

Pastor Spangenberg, can you comment on Luther's catechisms and his hymns? Our most honorable Doctor Luther composed an entire summary of Holy Scripture in specific question-and-answer form for the youth in an excellent work, his catechism. The instruction we have from him in the German language does not waste a word, and this golden little booklet is full of spirit and life, as the people who have read, heard, and meditated upon it with humility and reverence recognize. And it is not possible to praise his wonderful, enjoyable, and delightful German hymnal

5. Cochlaeus, *Historia*, 179a–80; *Luther's Lives*, 235–36.

sufficiently, for the hymns that are found in it as you page through it are suitable for your situation and your person. There are extremely beautiful doctrinal hymns and songs of comfort, and they can fortify a pious heart against all kinds of false teaching and error and give great comfort, lightening burdens of all kinds. It is a book that enriches the spirit if it's properly used.[6]

Doctor Luther, why did you decide to write your catechisms? The deplorable, wretched deprivation that I recently encountered while I was visiting the congregations in the countryside constrained and compelled me to prepare a catechism, or Christian instruction, in this kind of brief, plain, simple form. Dear God, what misery I beheld! The ordinary person, especially in the villages, knows absolutely nothing about the Christian faith, and unfortunately many pastors are completely unskilled and incompetent teachers. Yet supposedly they all bear the name Christian, are baptized, and receive the holy sacrament of the altar, even though they do not know the Lord's Prayer, the Creed, or the Ten Commandments! As a result they live like simple cattle or pigs who cannot think, and despite the fact that the gospel has returned, have mastered the art of misusing all their freedom.[7]

You taught the core of the Christian faith as you understand it with the help of the Apostles' Creed, and you divided it not according to the customary twelve "articles" of the centuries before your time, but instead you focused on the three persons of the Trinity and on the acts of God as creation, redemption, and sanctification. What did you teach the children to understand about God the Father and creation? They are to say, "I believe that God has created me together with all that exists. God has given me and still preserves my body

6. Spangenberg, *Warhafftiger Bericht*, C5a–b.
7. Small Catechism, BSELK 852/853; BC 347–48.

and soul: eyes, ears and all limbs and senses; reason and all mental faculties. In addition, God daily and abundantly provides shoes and clothing, food and drink, house and farm, spouse and children, fields, livestock and all property—along with all the necessities and nourishment for this body and life. God protects me against all danger and shields and preserves me from all evil. And all this is done out of pure, fatherly and divine goodness and mercy, without any merit or worthiness of mine at all! For all of this I owe it to God to thank and praise, serve and obey him. This is most certainly true."[8]

What were they to confess about Jesus and their deliverance from sin? "I believe that Jesus Christ, true God, begotten of the Father in eternity, and also a true human being, born of the Virgin Mary, is my LORD. He has redeemed me, a lost and condemned human being. He has purchased and freed me from all sins, from death, and from the power of the devil, not with gold or silver but with his holy, precious blood and with his innocent suffering and death. He has done all this in order that I may belong to him, live under him in his kingdom, and serve him in eternal righteousness, innocence and blessedness, just as he is risen from the dead and lives and rules eternally. This is most certainly true."[9]

And what did you want them to believe about the Holy Spirit? "I believe that by my own understanding or strength I cannot believe in Jesus Christ my LORD or come to him, but instead the Holy Spirit has called me through the gospel, enlightened me with his gifts, made me holy and kept me in the true faith, just as he calls, gathers, enlightens and makes holy the whole Christian church on earth and keeps it with Jesus Christ in the one common, true faith. Daily in this Christian church the Holy Spirit abundantly forgives

8. Small Catechism, BSELK 870/871; BC 354–55.
9. Small Catechism, BSELK 872/873; BC 355.

all sins—mine and those of all believers. On the last day the Holy Spirit will raise me and all the dead and will give to me and all believers in Christ eternal life. This is most certainly true."[10]

You concluded the instructional manual for children with Bible verses that related how they were to behave in their homes, in their economic service to society, in society in general, and in their congregations, and also how they should meditate on God's Word and pray each day. How did you suggest the day begin for Christians? By making the sign of the holy cross as a reminder of their baptisms, and then saying, "God the Father, Son and Holy Spirit watch over me. Amen . . .

I give thanks to you, my heavenly Father through Jesus Christ your dear Son, that you have protected me this night from all harm and danger, and I ask you that you would also protect me today from sin and all evil, so that my life and actions may please you completely. For into your hands I commend myself: my body, my soul and all that is mine. Let your holy angel be with me, so that the wicked foe may have no power over me. Amen."[11]

Doctor Cochlaeus, what is your estimate of Luther's catechisms? Although Luther, as if he were some kind of lawgiver and a new Moses, had written many things to his accomplices about the way in which they ought to teach and preach, both in his commentaries and in his *Instruction* for the Saxon visitation, nevertheless there remained such variety and discord among the preachers of his sect that it appeared necessary to him again to prescribe another rule for teaching, which he called the *Catechism*. In that book, in various passages he explained the Ten Commandments of God and the Lord's Prayer and the Apostles' Creed very

10. Small Catechism, BSELK 772/873; BC 355–56.
11. Small Catechism, BSELK 890/891; BC 363.

differently than he had done ten years earlier. For instance, he prescribed both belief in and use of two sacraments, namely, baptism and the eucharist, in a new manner, but he did not recognize any other sacraments. For although he urged the people to make confession in this book, still he regarded confession as something very different from what the holy mother church instituted. For he permitted the penitent person to mention not every sin that he knew he had committed but only those which he wanted to mention, so that he might receive counsel, consolation, and absolution from the priest. Subsequently, many people who had a high opinion of their worth followed Luther's example and published many catechisms. None of them agreed with any other in every detail. In this way they attempted to instill their dogma in boys and girls and the youth through bedtime stories, as if with the milk that they had drunk, so that strong roots, once planted in those tender breasts, would remain there through every stage of life and could not be eradicated through any force or argument. Thus, they wrote their catechisms most especially for children.[12]

Pastor Spalatin, please tell us a bit about the activities of Johannes Bugenhagen in aiding churches beyond Wittenberg in their efforts to reform. In 1528 Doctor Johann Bugenhagen, Pomeranus as we call him, the pastor in Wittenberg, was asked by the city council in Braunschweig to preach the gospel there for a period of time and to set aside unchristian ceremonies and establish Christian ceremonies. With the most gracious permission of Duke Johann of Saxony, the Elector, on the Sunday Rogate [the fifth Sunday after Easter], he arrived in Braunschweig and preached the gospel for a time, abolished the unchristian private masses and other unchristian ceremonies, and established in their place the Christian mass and other Christian ceremonies.

12. Cochlaeus, *Historia*, 190b; *Luther's Lives*, 246.

Also in 1528 the city council of Hamburg invited Doctor Johann Bugenhagen, Pomeranus, to come there. With the most gracious permission of the highly respected elector of Saxony, Duke Johann, he arrived in Hamburg on the festival of Saint Denis [October 9] and preached the gospel for a time, abolished unchristian masses and ceremonies, and established Christian masses and ceremonies, schools, and a hospital. In 1534 the cousins Dukes Barnim and Philipp of Pomerania held a diet of their nobles and towns, which was dedicated to the subject of the gospel. They requested the aid of their subject, Doctor Johannes Bugenhagen. In response to their invitation, with the most gracious permission of Duke Johann Friedrich, elector of Saxony, he arrived at their court on the festival of Saint Lucia. On the same day the honorable dukes agreed to accept the gospel and to permit the free and unhindered proclamation of the gospel in their principalities. The venerable Doctor Pomeranus preached the gospel in his fatherland, Pomerania, purely and clearly for a time. He abolished unchristian ceremonies, worship, and ordinances for the churches, and he established Christian masses, ceremonies, schools, a common chest, and a hospital.[13]

DISCUSSION QUESTIONS

1. Of Luther's publications for reshaping parish life and piety, which was the most important? Why?
2. Why did the sacraments become a focal point for dispute among those who rejected papal authority?

---

13. Spalatin, "Annales," 129–30, 297–98.

3. Why did both Elector Johann and the Wittenberg theologians think that the visitation of congregations in electoral Saxony was so important?

4. Why are Luther's catechisms often regarded as his most important publication?

5. How important for the spread of Luther's reform were the efforts of his colleague Johannes Bugenhagen?

FURTHER READING

1. The biographies and overviews of Luther's theology listed in the introduction.

2. Bornkamm, Heinrich. *Luther in Mid-Career, 1521–1530*. Edited, and with a foreword by Karin Bornkamm. Translated by E. Theodore Bachmann. Philadelphia: Fortress, 1983.

3. Sasse, Hermann. *This Is My Body: Luther's Contention for the Real Presence in the Sacrament of the Altar*. Minneapolis: Augsburg, 1959.

4. Burnett, Amy Nelson. *Debating the Sacraments: Print and Authority in the Early Reformation*. Oxford: Oxford University Press, 2019.

5. Vajta, Vilmos. *Luther on Worship*. Translated and condensed by U. S. Leupold. Philadelphia: Muhlenberg, 1958.

6. Wengert, Timothy J. *Law and Gospel: Philip Melanchthon's Debate with John Agricola of Eisleben over Poenitentia*. Texts and Studies in Reformation and Post-Reformation Thought. Grand Rapids: Baker, 1997.

7. Arand, Charles P. *That I May Be His Own: An Overview of Luther's Catechisms.* Saint Louis: Concordia Academic, 2000.

8. Hendel, Kurt K. ed. and trans. *Johannes Bugenhagen: Selected Writings.* 2 vols. Minneapolis: Fortress, 2015.

Chapter 8

The New Normal of the 1530s and 1540s

THE LODGING OF A *protestatio* did not establish a new "normal." Instead, it provoked Charles V to search for a new approach to ending the "Lutheran plague." He met in early 1530 with Pope Clement VII and then called for a new diet to meet in Augsburg. The Evangelical governments were to come there to explain and attempt to justify their deviations from established, legitimate medieval practice. The emperor hoped to induce the several towns and territories that were practicing Evangelical reform to return to the papal obedience. He was prepared to use more threats of force if necessary. In addition, Charles hoped that at the diet he could gain more tax money to fund his military action against the Turkish armies. They still posed a serious threat although they had just been hurled back from besieging Vienna.

Luther's supporters in those governments had sensed a worsening atmosphere in the empire. Therefore, in 1529 they had taken counsel to form a defensive league. At a meeting in the town of Schwabach they accepted a statement of faith drafted by Luther and his Wittenberg colleagues, the "Schwabach Articles." These articles summarized the doctrinal core of the Wittenberg theology. Representatives from electoral Saxony and Brandenburg-Ansbach accepted the "Articles" as the sufficient basis for a league dedicated to defending this teaching. The implications for practice were not developed in this document.

Another critical meeting took place about the same time, aimed at preparing the way for such a league. Landgrave Philip of Hesse hoped to reconcile Luther, Melanchthon, Johann Brenz (the chief south German reformer and supporter of Wittenberg theology), and their associates with the Swiss delegation in order to expand the league. He invited all sides to a colloquy at his castle in Marburg in autumn 1529. The conversations went better than anticipated, but they failed to bridge the gap between the parties regarding the presence of Christ's body and blood in the Lord's Supper. The participants agreed on fourteen articles of faith, but sufficient accord on the sacrament of the altar and the presence of Christ in the elements of bread and wine eluded them. Consequently, the Swiss remained aloof from the German governments who in 1531 formed the Smalcald League.

In the following months, in anticipation of the diet in Augsburg, Elector Johann commissioned his theologians in Wittenberg to draft a statement explaining the reforms that the Saxon government had introduced and the biblical justification for them. Since the eighteenth century the term "Torgau Articles" has been used for one or another draft treating specific reform measures. We still are not certain, however, precisely which of these drafts Melanchthon took with him to Augsburg. When he arrived there, he found that Johann Eck of Ingolstadt had petitioned the emperor to permit a disputation on "Four Hundred Four Articles" or theses. Eck had mixed together accurate and inaccurate citations from the Wittenberg theologians, along with quotations of similar quality from many of those whom Luther and Melanchthon opposed, but who were also in rebellion against the Roman pope. Melanchthon perceived the need to do more than explain reform measures as he and his colleagues had planned. He felt compelled to assert the catholic nature and biblical faithfulness of his and Luther's teaching in general.

Luther could not accompany his colleagues to Augsburg if he wished to avoid being burned at the stake. He and Melanchthon formulated a pair of goals that they hoped negotiations and testimony could accomplish. They planned to give a clear confession of their faith—their understanding of the biblical message—and they planned to seek reconciliation with the emperor and the bishops of the Roman obedience. Melanchthon and his colleagues from Wittenberg and other Evangelical lands and towns spent weeks in tough, tense conversations with the theologians in imperial service. Melanchthon made great efforts to reach reconciliation while drafting a simple but clear confession of the faith and explanation of reforms. He had help from both theological and secular counselors of the Evangelical governments. He had high hopes of some sort of reconciliation and a plan for peace. His colleague, Justus Jonas, also present in Augsburg, was less sanguine about that possibility but supported Melanchthon's confession.

Melanchthon's draft of the position of the "protesting" princes and towns was read to the emperor on June 25, 1530, in the presence of the entire diet. It contains twenty-one brief articles on topics of biblical teaching. They aimed at demonstrating that Wittenberg teaching was faithful to Scripture and the catholic tradition of the church. It also contained seven articles detailing reasons for the reform of pious practices, including marriage of priests, fasting,

The New Normal of the 1530s and 1540s

confession and absolution, the mass, monasticism, and the power of bishops and the nature of their office. Charles did not understand German. He fell asleep while the booming voice of Saxon co-chancellor Christian Beyer broadcast the confession to the participants in the diet and to the crowds outside the hall. They did not fall asleep. They understood and delighted in what they believed to be the clear assertion of biblical faithfulness and adherence to the universal tradition of the church contained in this Augsburg Confession. Luther also, despite some reservations, approved and applauded Melanchthon's work. He observed that the composition of such a document was a task for the tactful colleague rather than his own tempestuous spirit.

Charles and Ferdinand were not impressed. They organized a committee of their own advisors to refute the Evangelical confession. Johann Eck was one of the leading contributors, along with other prominent German theologians and Spanish counselors. The emperor recognized that the harsh tone and blanket condemnation contained in their first effort could only exacerbate the situation. He sent them back to the drawing board. On August 3, 1530, their "confutation"—labeled by its critics "the Papal Confutation" although the papal curia wanted nothing to do with it—was read to and accepted by the emperor as an adequate justification for moving militarily against the Evangelical governments. He set the date for their compliance with the Edict of Worms and return to papal obedience at April 15, 1531.

Other distractions diverted Charles's attention; he was still beset by enemies on several fronts at or beyond the empire's borders. Therefore, in 1532 the imperial government negotiated a truce, "the Nuremberg Armistice." This permitted the Smalcald League to continue its Evangelical practices and, in fact, expand. The truce was renewed in "the Frankfurt Armistice" of 1539. By the end of the 1530s intense efforts at reconciliation of Evangelicals and those faithful to Rome gained ground. In 1540 and 1541, in meetings held in Hagenau, Worms, and Regensburg, a religious colloquy took place. Gasparo Cardinal Contarini of Venice joined German Roman Catholic theologians in conversations with Melanchthon, Martin Bucer of Strassburg, and others. They produced a common statement on justification by faith. It pleased almost no one. Hoped-for reconciliation eluded the negotiators. The emperor resolved to pursue a military solution. He waged his pursuit of that solution on the battlefield after another diet in Regensburg in 1546 had produced nothing there: Roman Catholic participation in another dialogue on religious issues was halfhearted.

However, in the closing years of Luther's life the Nuremberg and Frankfurt Armistice agreements ensured a relatively stable situation for Luther's adherents, still illegal but not immediately threatened. Therefore, more territorial and municipal rulers formally attached their lands to the Smalcald League. For the Wittenberg team, now increased by the addition of former student and Magdeburg school rector Caspar Cruciger, a new normal took shape.

Scholars have long debated whether Melanchthon and Luther shared the same understanding of the message of Holy Scripture. After Luther's death some of the brightest and best of their students found that Melanchthon was straying from Luther's teaching on the freedom of the will and the Lord's Supper. Luther never noticed any significant differences in their understanding of the biblical message even though he must have recognized that they expressed their common teaching in different ways. Their different accents arose out differing backgrounds, personalities, spiritual histories, and assignments at the university and in electoral service. Melanchthon served the Saxon electors

The New Normal of the 1530s and 1540s

and the Smalcald League as an ecclesiastical and theological diplomat. The weight of the defense of Wittenberg theology at the imperial level lay on his shoulders. This shaped his formulation of that teaching at times as he tried to find formulations of the biblical truths upon which both sides could agree.

Some nineteenth-century and early twentieth-century theologians misinterpreted Luther's doctrine of justification to fit it into their own systems of thought. They regarded Luther's doctrine of the justification of the sinner to be different from Melanchthon's. It was not. It is clear that Luther, like Melanchthon, taught that God's gift of righteousness comes "forensically," that is, by the pronouncement of the almighty, re-creative Word of God, and takes form first of all in faith. It is also true that Luther was just as concerned as Melanchthon about new obedience that flows from trusting Christ. Both believed that God as Creator is almighty and responsible for everything in his creation. Both believed that human beings, created in God's image, are held responsible for trusting and obeying him. Unlike most other theologians, they did not try to divide the role of grace and the role of human works in some mathematical manner. Instead, they held the two total responsibilities—divine and human—in tension, addressing the existential human situation with their distinction of law and gospel.

Within the context of addressing specific situations and questions with either law or gospel, Melanchthon's alleged crediting of some freedom to the sinful human will to turn itself to God is a false reading of what Melanchthon wrote on the subject, for he emphasizes that the will functions only under the "drawing" or empowerment of the Holy Spirit. Only in his view of the true presence of Christ's body and blood in the Lord's Supper do Melanchthon's ways of expressing his teaching raise questions in the last years of his life concerning whether he did not indeed depart from the substance of Luther's position, although he always affirmed the presence of Christ and the saving promise conveyed in the sacrament.

Continuing bouts with illness often incapacitated Luther for shorter or longer periods beginning in the late 1520s. Nonetheless, he took part in the bustling life around him. The Black Cloister continued to be full of students and others who needed shelter from the storms of life. Luther gave them personal support and counsel. Despite one physical malady or another and in the face of bouts of melancholy, the professor functioned as a public teacher not only through his lectures and sermons but also through his letters and memoranda. These memoranda were prepared with his colleagues for the church and for secular rulers from the German lands and beyond. He counseled and consoled kings, dukes, counts, nobles, pastors and patricians, merchants and artisans, from throughout the empire and across western Europe. Bugenhagen's travels to aid in organizing churches in lands introducing Lutheran reforms gave Luther many opportunities to preach in Wittenberg's town church. His lectures formed the heart of his life. His writing occupied much of his time.

These years saw the production of significant theological works. Most influential and most appreciated by his students were his published lectures on Galatians (1531) and Genesis (1535–1545) as well as on selected psalms (1530–1535) and portions of Isaiah (1529, 1543, 1544). Genesis gave him rich opportunity to use his gift of storytelling. The narratives of the patriarchs offered him material to personify doctrinal positions and to model behavior faithful to God's plan for human living. Elector Johann Friedrich, who succeeded his father Johann in 1532, commissioned the deacon from the Wittenberg town church,

The New Normal of the 1530s and 1540s

Georg Rörer, to serve formally as recorder of the professor's public utterances. Rörer had been taking careful, extensive notes on Luther's sermons and lectures for some years. In 1539 the elector commissioned him to edit his mentor's complete works. Caspar Cruciger turned to editing other sermons, including a new church postil. Luther's sermons to the household at the Cloister were also redacted and issued as a postil to aid pastors in their preaching.

In late May 1536 Melanchthon drew Luther into formal conversation with Martin Bucer of Strassburg and other south German pastors. These theologians had been reluctant to accept Luther's "true presence" of Christ's body and blood in the Lord's Supper, but they did believe that Christ was present in the sacrament in a spiritual manner. Melanchthon's "Wittenberg Concord" provided common language. Bucer accepted Luther's description of the true presence of Christ's body and blood as a "sacramental presence," and the preposition "with" to describe the relationship of his body and blood to the bread and wine. They agreed that the "unworthy" receive Christ's body and blood sacramentally because of the promise of the words of institution of the Supper. Bucer subsequently sent students to Wittenberg for preparation for the pastorate in Strassburg.

In late 1536 Elector Johann Friedrich asked Luther to prepare a statement to guide representatives of the Smalcald League in testifying to their faith at the council that Pope Paul II had called for Mantua for May 1537. The elector had been pressing Luther to write a theological "last will and testament." He wanted a document that would reinforce a statement of the core of this teaching like that which Luther had appended to his *Confession on the Lord's Supper* of 1528. Luther assembled a small committee to aid him, adding Amsdorf, Agricola, and Spalatin to his four Wittenberg colleagues. In fact, he worked largely alone and drafted what came to be known as "the Smalcald Articles." These "Articles" provided bullet points in German for princes and town council members to use in discussing issues with Roman Catholic theologians at the council. The League decided to use the Augsburg Confession as its basic position paper, along with a "Treatise on the Power and Primacy of the Pope" drawn up by Melanchthon at the League's meeting in February 1537, but attending theologians subscribed to Luther's "Articles." This document became, with the Augsburg Confession, a standard for public teaching in Lutheran churches over the next quarter century.

Johann Agricola stood again at the center of the first open conflict within Wittenberg ranks. Agricola had demonstrated many skills and insights as a student of Luther's in the 1510s. He had remained in Wittenberg until he assumed the rectorate of the school in his native Eisleben in 1525. As discussed above (ch. 7), Agricola had caught from Luther and later from Melanchthon that the law is the sinner's enemy and that the gospel rescues believers from the condemnation of the law. He did not absorb the insistence of the two that, like Paul in Romans 7, baptized Christians are plagued by the mystery of the continuation of sin and evil in their lives. He rejected the necessity of a continuing role for the law to call believers to daily repentance.

After coming to Wittenberg to aid in the composition of the Smalcald Articles, Agricola remained in the town. Luther arranged for him to teach at the university, and Agricola revived his ideas regarding the law's playing no role in the Christian life. Luther rejected this position. It contradicted his perception of the necessity of distinguishing law and gospel. He feared that Agricola was undercutting the proper call for repentance, the recognition that believers remain in the struggle against sin, and thus the consolation of the gospel. After Agricola announced several times

The New Normal of the 1530s and 1540s

that he was abandoning his position but then continued to teach it to his students and preach it anyway, Luther conducted disputations on "antinomianism" in 1537 and 1538, repudiating Agricola's theology. Elector Johann Friedrich forbade Agricola to leave Wittenberg until the matter could be resolved. Agricola secretly departed and assumed a position as court preacher at the court of Elector Joachim II of Brandenburg.

The pending papal council, which finally met in Trent in 1545, also gave Luther occasion to compose a longer treatise *On the Councils and the Church* in 1539, picking up themes he had treated in his *On the Three Symbols or Creeds of the Christian Church* (1538) and anticipating a fierce polemic against the duke of Braunschweig-Wolfenbüttel, Heinrich the Younger. Heinrich had burned the town of Einbeck in order to bring it back to Roman obedience and into his own territory, and he had publicly insulted Elector Johann Friedrich. Luther responded with a satirical review of Heinrich's misdeeds, *Against Hans Wurst* in 1541 (Hans Wurst was a fool figure in popular literature), repeating and expanding ideas from *On the Councils and the Church*. These three treatises—*On the Councils and the Church*, *On the Three Symbols*, and *Against Hans Wurst*—summarized Luther's doctrine of the church.

Biblical interpretation formed the foundation of Luther's engagement in the ongoing discussions, mostly polemical and harsh, with Roman Catholic opponents, with Anabaptists, and with Jews—particularly Jewish interpreters of the Old Testament. Luther's early comments on the only significant non-Christian minority in medieval German lands, the Jews, expressed hope that once papal teaching had been set aside, they would accept Christ as Messiah. His *That Jesus Christ was Born a Jew* of 1523, a defense of the virgin birth of Jesus, set forth his expectation and desire that many would convert to a purified Christian church. Although this did not happen on any extensive scale, Luther continued to encourage pastors who were given the opportunity to baptize interested Jewish adults. Frequently in his lectures on Old Testament books, he engaged Jewish biblical interpreters. Their failure to see certain passages as prophecies of the Messiah's birth as Jesus of Nazareth and to acknowledge the teaching of the Trinity in other verses disturbed Luther profoundly. Katharina, her worldview formed by an upbringing in the lower nobility, which often had unfortunate encounters with Jewish lenders, reinforced any negative disposition Martin might have had.

Particularly crucial for his turning with a sinful fury against the Jewish population that had not accepted Christ were rumors in the early 1540s, passed on by trusted friends in Bohemia and others, that Jews were trying to convert Christians. His belief that Satan was attacking the church with special vigor because Christ's return was imminent led Luther to issue *On the Jews and Their Lies* in 1543. This work blemishes his reputation because it exhibits the worst of widespread feeling against the Jews in late medieval Europe.

Alongside other activities in the last years of Luther's life was the continuing teamwork on his translation of the Bible. After the appearance of his New Testament in translation in 1522, he assembled his Wittenberg colleagues and others to produce a German Old Testament. Luther took the lead in the struggle with Hebrew words and grammar. He consulted with local butchers about names for animal body parts in Leviticus and with courtiers in electoral service about military terms. He also relied heavily on the linguistic skills of Melanchthon, Jonas, Hebrew professor Matthäus Aurogallus, and others to find just the right expressions to convey the prophets' meaning. The Pentateuch appeared in

The New Normal of the 1530s and 1540s

print in 1523, the books from Joshua to Ecclesiastes had come out in two volumes during 1524. The prophetic books followed in 1532, and the translation of the Apocrypha was completed in order to make possible the publication of the entire Bible in one volume in 1534. All the while, the New Testament was subject to ongoing revision. By Luther's death, an estimated half million copies of parts or all of his German Bible had been printed and sold.

Luther had expected death for many years, in the 1520s at the hand of pope or emperor; by the end of the 1520s through one of the many sicknesses that troubled his stomach, heart, and head. In late 1545, days after completing his Genesis lectures, he journeyed to his birthplace, Eisleben, to negotiate a reconciliation among the counts of his native Mansfeld, brothers and cousins. They refined the art of princely antagonism to exceptional heights. He returned to Wittenberg at the end of December and then in late January traveled back to Eisleben with his three sons, who visited family in the area, and his student secretary, Johannes Aurifaber. His former colleague and close friend Justus Jonas, who had left Wittenberg in 1541 to introduce reform in the city of Halle, joined them. Luther's efforts concluded in at least a temporary truce for the counts.

This trip also claimed his life. The fourth sermon he preached in two weeks in Eisleben was cut short by exhaustion. On the evening of February 17, he suffered a heart attack. He prayed Psalm 31:6, "I hate those who look to worthless idols, but I trust in the Lord." In the earliest hours of February 18, he used Simeon's words in Luke 2:29, "Lord, now let your servant depart in peace according to your Word," to depart this life. Less than forty-eight hours earlier, he had written of the need for long experience in pastoral care to truly minister to God's people with his Word, ending his brief note, "We are beggars. That is the truth."

The beggar before the Lord returned in his casket in a triumphal procession to Wittenberg. Melanchthon delivered a funeral oration. Bugenhagen preached a funeral sermon. Luther was laid to rest in the Castle church, in which he had preached and taught. His students continued his preaching and teaching. His life and his message continues to inspire and guide Christians in many corners of the world to this day.

INTERVIEWS

Doctor Luther, how did you see the negotiations at Marburg? We agreed on almost all points except that our opponents remain committed to the view that it is only bread in the Lord's Supper, and they maintain that Christ is only spiritually present. The landgrave wanted us to negotiate with the intention that we come to agreement, and that if we continue to disagree, we would still accept each other as brothers and as members of Christ. The landgrave really wanted us to put some effort into this. But we did not want that kind of "brother" and "member." We wanted peace, but we also wanted the best for everyone.[1]

Pastor Spalatin, you were there as the Augsburg Confession was presented to Emperor Charles on June 25, 1530. Please give us your impressions. That Saturday, the evening of the festival of Saint John the Holy Baptist, the most important event that has ever taken place on earth took place. On the afternoon of that day my most gracious lord, the Elector of Saxony, Duke Johann, Margrave George of Brandenburg[-Ansbach], Duke Johann Friedrich of Saxony, Duke Ernst of Braunschweig and Lüneburg, Landgrave Philip of Hesse, Duke Franz of Braunschweig and Lüneburg, Prince Wolfgang of Anhalt, and the cities of

1. WA Br 5:154, Nr. 1476.

The New Normal of the 1530s and 1540s

Nuremberg and Reutlingen made public confession of the faith and the entire Christian teaching that they had had preached in their principalities, lands, and cities. They had it read in German with a Christian, noble, and confident spirit and heart, article by article, not only to all the electors, princes, nobles, bishops, and counselors who were present but especially to the Roman imperial majesty himself and his brother King Ferdinand. The chancellor of Saxony, Doctor Christian Beyer, read it, and he read it very clearly and loudly, so that not only those in the hall itself, where the diet was being conducted, heard it, but also those who were standing below in the courtyard of the bishop of Augsburg, where his imperial majesty was staying, were listening as it was being read. And this confession had been composed in German and Latin but for the sake of time was read only in German. In both Latin and German this confession was certainly composed with the Holy Scriptures as its basis and in such a conciliatory tone that there is no other confession in a thousand years like it, and there will not be anything similar so long as the world stands, with which to compare it. There is nothing in the histories nor by any of the ancient teachers like it.[2]

Pastor Myconius, what happened after the presentation of the Augsburg Confession to Emperor Charles? After that, the theologians from the two sides were ordered to seek concord. There were also princes involved. But Eck and the other sophists remained sophists. Then it was commanded that the papists should refute our articles of faith in writing. They proceeded to do so. The entire empire was in suspense several months and waited for them to do something positive. When the document was ready, it was given to the emperor and the representatives from throughout the empire, but it was not good for boiling or roasting. They wanted the

2. Spalatin, "Annales," 134–35.

Evangelicals to take an oath before they had seen the document that they would accept it, believe it, and hold to its teachings, and certainly not let it out to the common people or write against it or oppose it in any way. In that way they wanted to end the matter. Such foolish presumption had never been heard of. Thus, it was not made public, but it was kept secret in whatever ways were possible. Some of the tyrants, particularly the German cardinals and bishops, were plotting to summon the princes who accepted the Augsburg Confession secretly to the emperor's quarters, seize them, and behead them. But they were afraid of an open revolt. They feared that the murderers would reap a terrible reward. Nonetheless, Landgrave Philip of Hesse rode away in secret. That made the papists rather lose heart. But Margrave Joachim of Brandenburg, the elector, was sent to the elector of Saxony and the adherents of the Augsburg Confession to persuade them that they should abandon their confession and should adhere to the teaching of the Roman church, its obedience, and its regulations—that is, the deception of the pope, his blasphemy and mischief. If they refused, the elector said, the imperial royal majesty and empire would move against him with military might. Body and life, property and blood would be on the line, the elector threatened. The pious, praiseworthy elector, Duke Johann, answered, "Well, now, I would not have anticipated that such a clear presentation of the holy Christian faith would meet with such harshness and such a devious response, but I will not, if God grant it, deny my dear God and the Lord Christ for the sake of the emperor, the empire, or any human being. And what would it help me, if I gained the favor of the whole world and lost God's favor? You, dear God, protect me from doing that." Two days later the pious praiseworthy prince went home. In 1531 the Apology of the Confession and a new *Loci Communes* appeared in print.

The New Normal of the 1530s and 1540s

[In fact, the second edition of the *Loci communes* was published in 1535.] The admirable martyr or witness of Christ, Philip Melanchthon, composed them. His books have accomplished much good among learned people in the whole world and lay out the true foundation of our teaching.[3]

Pastor Spangenberg, you heard Luther lecture toward the end of his life. What was your impression? Everyone who heard him knows what kind of man Luther was when he preached or lectured at the university. Shortly before his death he lectured on . . . Genesis. What sheer genius, life, and power he had! The way he could say it! . . . in my entire life I have experienced nothing more inspiring. When I heard his lectures, it was as if I were hearing an angel of the Lord . . . Luther had a great command of Scripture and sensed its proper meaning at every point. Dear God, there was a gigantic gift of being able to interpret Scripture properly in that man.[4]

Pastor Mathesius, can you comment on Luther as a lecturer? You experienced his lectures on Genesis. Our Doctor proved himself to be a prophet of God, a servant of Jesus Christ, and an interpreter of Holy Scripture, from which he brought us much blessed teaching on patience and comfort and sure hope. . . . Whoever wants to learn of Christ in Genesis and receive the message of the power of the living Word of God and what sin is and the righteousness that counts in God's sight should read [Luther's commentary on Genesis]. So should those who want to grasp the comfort of hope in him and how to remain faithful to our God and be strengthened by him in times of anxiety and oppression. It will help a person grasp how to use the failings and faith of the great saints. [The commentary reveals] what the teacher [Luther] sees in Scripture and to what we

3. Myconius, "Historia," 93–94.

4. Spangenberg, *Theander Lutherus*, 70a–b.

should pay attention, so we readers are able to convey to our hearers and apply it to their lives so that they can make it their own. It helps particularly when we are caught under the holy cross and falling into the opinion that God is not present and has completely forgotten us. Such a person will find in his Genesis commentary what our elderly Doctor experienced in the temptations of his last days and brought together in this book. I am bequeathing what I think of this blessed commentary to my children and members of my congregation so that they do not forget and learn to respect their entire lives how wonderful and precious this commentary is. Then they will be able to share its usefulness for all matters in the church . . . Pay attention to this exposition, which explains Christ's words and will, through which God has proclaimed comfort, rest, and life to my torn and troubled heart. For when our situations are like those of the crosses of the patriarchs, this exposition [of Genesis] hits our heart, as the Doctor really speaks it to us. That is how the commentator loves and lives and refreshes and quickens the heart.[5]

Pastor Spalatin, you knew Johann Agricola from the 1510s on and were often together with him. What led to the break between him and Luther? In 1537 the poisonous, devilish teaching and error of the Antinomians gained prominence. They taught, as opponents of the law, that only the gospel, not the law, should be preached. Especially Master Johann Agricola from Eisleben and a few others taught that. Agricola did that despite the fact that he had been trained in the Christian school at Wittenberg. They pushed this teaching somewhat sneakily, not so much in public, but really caused a great harm. This deeply troubled our dear father, Doctor Martin Luther. Although he through others and especially through the provost of the Castle church, Doctor

5. Mathesius, *Historien*, CLXXXa–CLXXXIa.

The New Normal of the 1530s and 1540s

Justus Jonas, warned against this error in a Christian missive to Agricola, which I myself read, nothing seemed to help. Agricola went around spreading his opinion, dangerous and wrong as it was, in Eisleben, Mansfeld, Wittenberg, and other locations among many people. At this time Doctor Martin Luther preached strongly against his opinion, and he conducted several excellent disputations against it. In one disputation Agricola was challenged to argue against him, and he expressed regret for his error, but he still did not abandon it in his heart. That caused Doctor Martin Luther to forbid him to preach so that he would no longer cave in to this dangerous, erroneous teaching, which cultivated nothing but secure, rebellious, criminal people, who lived without any fear of God, shame, or hesitation, like animals without reason. For such sweet teaching pleases the crowd, our flesh and blood, a great deal, for they can tolerate neither law nor reprimand.[6]

Pastor Spalatin, you have noted how the Wittenberg reform was spreading in the German Empire and among its government officials in the 1530s and 1540s. What are examples of this? In 1539 the holy gospel punched a big hole in the devil's kingdom, no matter how intensively the devil with his henchmen and those who serve as his instruments caused confusion, practiced oppression, threatened, raged, and growled. Even with poison, bribes, and promises he continued to do so. Margrave Joachim II, elector of Brandenburg, and his brother Margrave Johannes, accepted the precious gospel and the Christian mass and communion. Joachim sought out good, learned Christian preachers and permitted the gospel to be preached freely, purely, and publicly. In intense negotiations, Elector Joachim dealt with the three bishops [with jurisdictions in his lands], of Brandenburg, Lebus, and Havelberg, in a Christian manner: The

6. Spalatin, "Annales," 311–12.

bishop of Brandenburg quickly behaved in a proper, Christian manner as I heard from Doctor Martin Luther. After his father-in-law, King Sigismund of Poland, wrote Joachim a harsh reprimand at the instigation of certain people, the elector asked Philip Melanchthon to come to Berlin, and he responded with such a forthright, good, honorable Christian answer. In it he conceded nothing of the gospel but in a friendly tone, with respectful pleas, promised with God's help not to introduce any unchristian teaching or ceremonies until the council should meet and to act only in a Christian and irreproachable manner. In 1542 Almighty God, in his fatherly goodness, brought his Word even further. Duke Ott-Heinrich of Bavaria [in this case, the Palatinate, which belonged to the traditional domains of the Wittelsbach family, the dukes of Bavaria], son of Duke Ruprecht of Bavaria, issued a public edict and regulation for all the clergy and subjects in his domains, that they accept God's Word and permit it to be freely preached and taught. With a gracious Christian desire and encouragement, they were to follow Christian teaching in their way of life and conduct. If some should demonstrate that they lacked something in their doctrine and understanding, they should consult learned theologians and obtain instruction and tutoring without any hesitation.[7]

Pastor Myconius, please describe the relationship of Wittenberg with Strassburg. There were excellent people there from the very beginning, and this praiseworthy municipality above all others has done much for the confession of the gospel and for learned studies. The father of all this was Jacob Sturm, the leader of the city council. The entire empire loved and praised this man's honesty and skill in all the arts, his upright conduct, his wisdom, and his reliability. Martin Bucer was an insightful, learned, and engaged man:

7. Spalatin, "Annales," 368–69, 671.

The New Normal of the 1530s and 1540s

his writings are still available. At first, he was burned by a false view of the sacraments, but he publicly laid that aside in Wittenberg in 1536.[8]

Professor Melanchthon, what did you tell the student body when you learned of Luther's death? I said, "A little before dinner on Wednesday, February 17, Doctor Luther began to contend with his frequent illness, the pressure of humors in the stomach—I remember his suffering this a number of times. The pain returned after dinner, so in his discomfort he sought to be alone in the nearby bedroom. He slept for close to two hours until the pains increased. Since Doctor Jonas was sleeping along with him in the same room, Doctor Martin called and woke him, told him to get up and make sure that Ambrose, the tutor of his children, heat the living room since he wanted to go into it. Soon Count Albert from the ruling Mansfeld family came there with his wife and many others . . . At last when Luther sensed that the end of his life was near, before 4 a.m. on February 18, he commended himself to God with this prayer: "My heavenly Father, eternal merciful God, you have revealed to me your beloved Son, our Lord Jesus Christ, whom I have known and with whom I have become familiar, whom I love and honor as my beloved Savior and Redeemer, whom the godless persecute, pursue, and reprove. Take my soul to you." Then he said three times, "Into your hands I commend my spirit [Luke 23:46]. You have redeemed me, God of truth [Ps 31:5]." And "God so loved the world that he gave his only begotten Son, that whoever believes shall be saved [John 3:16]." After repeating these prayers several times, he was called by God into the everlasting academy and into everlasting joys, in which he enjoys the company of the Father, Son, and Holy Spirit, and of all the prophets and apostles. Oh, the charioteer and the chariot of Israel

---

8. Myconius, "Historia," 62.

[1 Kgs 2:12, a comparison of the prophet Elijah's departure from the world with Luther's] has died. He guided the church in this last age of the world, for the doctrine of the forgiveness of sins and the promise of the Son of God was not apprehended by human wisdom. It was revealed by God through this man, whom we saw was raised up by God himself. Therefore, let us cherish the memory of this man and the teaching he has handed down to us, and let us think on the tremendous calamities and changes that will follow his death."[9]

Pastor Spangenberg, what is your appraisal of your mentor? It was Luther's way of communicating when he dealt with religious matters to go to the root cause carefully and surely because he spoke so well in the language of the apostles and at all times pointed to our dear Christ and showed the true way to heaven. He also destroyed the assaults and every power that opposed the true knowledge of God. He took all reasoning captive under obedience to Christ. His theology and writings can rightfully and truly be called David's slingshot, Paul's mouth, John's writing hand, Peter's key, and the sword of the Holy Spirit. To sum it all up, he had internalized our dear Paul, who had received his witness from God, so powerfully that you could only hear Paul when Luther spoke.[10]

DISCUSSION QUESTIONS

1. What made the Augsburg Confession so important for Luther's followers?
2. Compare the importance or significance of the fifteen years in Luther's life between 1515 and 1530 with the

---

9. CR 6:58–59.
10. Spangenberg, *Warhafftiger Bericht*, A8b.

importance or significance of the fifteen years between 1530 and his death.

3. How did changing circumstances in the last years of his life influence Luther's public utterances on those whom he saw as foes of the gospel, including the Jews?

4. What aspects of Luther's calling as a professor assumed importance in this period?

5. Comment on Melanchthon's reaction to Luther's death. What does it tell about the relationship between the two colleagues?

FURTHER READING

1. Bornkamm, Heinrich. *Luther in Mid-Career, 1521–1530*. Edited, and with a foreword by Karin Bornkamm. Translated by E. Theodore Bachmann. Philadelphia: Fortress, 1983.

2. Edwards, Mark U., Jr. *Luther and the False Brethren*. Stanford: Stanford University Press, 1975.

3. Edwards, Mark U., Jr. *Luther's Last Battles: Politics and Polemics, 1531–46*. Ithaca: Cornell University Press, 1983.

4. Arand Charles P., et al. *The Lutheran Confessions: History and Theology of the Book of Concord*. Minneapolis: Fortress, 2012.

5. Brady, Thomas. *The Politics of the Reformation in Germany: Jacob Sturm (1489–1553) of Strasbourg*. Atlantic Highlands, NJ: Humanities, 1997.

6. Kolb, Robert. *Luther and the Stories of God: Biblical Narratives as a Foundation for Christian Living*. Grand Rapids: Baker Academic, 2012.

7. Jenson, Gordon A. *The Wittenberg Concord: Creating Space for Dialogue*. Lutheran Quarterly Books. Minneapolis: Fortress, 2018.

Index of Persons

Adrian VI (Adriaan Floriszn Boeyens), pope, 83
Aemilius, Georg, 11
Agricola, Johann, 125–27, 149–51, 158–59
Albert the Great, 46
Albert, count of Mansfeld, 161
Albert, duke of Saxony, 21
Albrecht of Hohenzollern, archbishop of Mainz, 57–59, 69
Aleander, Girolamo, 83–84, 92
Amsdorf, Nikolaus von, 56, 85–87, 90, 106, 149
Aristotle, 16, 24–26, 33, 37–38, 45–46, 56
Augustine, 21, 25, 29–30, 38, 41, 47, 49, 55–56, 73, 77, 99
Aurifaber, Johannes, 153
Aurogallus, Matthäus, 152

Barnim, duke of Pomerania, 139
Baumgartner, Hieronymus, 106
Beier, Leonhard, 62
Benedict, Georg, xii
Bernard of Clairvaux, 23–24, 29, 31–32
Bernhardi, Bernard, 55, 62
Beyer, Christian, 145, 155
Biel, Gabriel, 24–25, 29, 37, 55
Bora, Magdalena von, 107
Braun, Johannes, 7
Brenz, Johannes, 105, 124, 127, 143
Brück, Gregor, 130
Bucer, Martin, xii, 73, 146, 149, 160–61
Bugenhagen, Johannes, 89–90, 102, 127, 138–39, 148, 154

Cajetan, Thomas de Vio, cardinal, 58, 63, 73–74
Campanus, Johann, 132
Charles V of Habsburg, emperor, 48, 81–85, 91, 93, 95, 97, 129–30, 142–46, 154–56
Cicero, 14, 39
Cochlaeus, Johannes, xii

Index of Persons

Contarini, Gasparo, cardinal, 146
Cotta, Kunz von, 6
Cotta, Ursula von, 6
Cranach, Lukas, 60, 131
Cruciger, Caspar, 146, 149

Demosthenes, 39
Dietrich, Veit, xiii
Donatus, Aelius, 9, 10
Duns Scotus, Joannes, 30, 46, 73

Eck, Johann (Ingolstadt), 61, 63–65, 74–78, 81 143–45, 155
Eck, Johann (Trier), 84
Elisabeth of Denmark, electress of Brandenburg, 107
Erasmus, Desiderius, of Rotterdam, 39–41, 62, 73, 83, 87, 91–92, 102, 104, 108–9, 112–14
Ernst, duke of Braunschweig-Lüneburg, 154
Ernst, elector of Saxony, 21

Francis I, king of France, 82–83
Ferdinand, king of Aragon, 82
Ferdinand, duke of Austria, king, 75, 130, 145, 155
Franz, duke of Braunschweig-Lüneburg, 154

Franz von Waldeck, bishop of Münster, 125
Frederick II, elector of Saxony, 21
Frederick III, the Wise, elector of Saxony, xii, xv, 21, 42, 57–59, 61, 63–64, 66, 70, 83–84, 86, 88–89, 91–92, 97, 101, 105–6
Froben, Johannes, 40

Georg, duke of Saxony, xii, 63, 90, 105, 131
George, margrave of Brandenburg-Ansbach, 154
Glatz, Caspar, 106
Grumbach, Argula von, 107
Günther, Franz, 56, 62
Gutenberg, Johannes, 59

Heinrich the younger, duke of Braunschweig-Wolfenbüttel, 151
Henry VIII, king of England, 90
Hermann of Schildesche, 19
Hilten, Johann, 6, 15
Hoffmeister, Johannes, xiii
Hubmayer, Balthasar, 132
Hus, Jan/Johann, 30, 63–64, 76, 83, 95

Isabella, queen of Leon and Castile, 82

Joachim I, elector of Brandenburg, 57, 61, 107, 156

Index of Persons

Joachim II, elector of Brandenburg, 107, 151, 159–60
Joanna of Aragon, 82
Johann, elector of Saxony, 101, 106, 126, 130, 138–39, 143, 148, 154, 156
Johann Friedrich, elector of Saxony, 139, 148–49, 151, 154
Johannes, margrave of Brandenburg, 159
Jonas, Justus, 90, 102, 117, 144, 152–53, 159, 161
Jonas, Justus, Jr., 117
Jud, Leo, 104

Karlstadt, Andreas Bodenstein von, 35, 55–56, 63, 75, 77, 87–90, 106, 123, 132
Koppe, Leonhard, 102

Ladislaus (Louis) II, king of Hungary, 82, 97–98
Lang, Johannes, 22, 112
Latomus, Jacob (Masson), 65
Lefèvre D'Étaples, Jacques, 39
Leiden, Jan van, 125
Leo X, pope, 57–58, 62–64, 68–69, 71, 81
Linck, Wenceslaus, 22
Luder, Hans, 1–5, 8–11, 19–20, 115
Luder, Margarete (Lindemann), 1–2, 5, 11
Lufft, Hans, 109
Luther, Elisabeth, 107, 117
Luther, Hans, 107–108, 116–17
Luther, Katharina (von Bora), 9, 106–7, 118, 152
Luther, Magdalena, 107–8, 117–18
Luther, Margarethe, 107
Luther, Martin, Jr., 107
Luther, Paul, 107

Mary of Burgundy, empress, 82
Mary of Habsburg, queen of Hungary, 82
Mathesius, Johannes xiii
Mathijs, Jan, 125
Maximilian I of Habsburg, emperor, 66, 81–82
Melanchthon, Philip, xiii, 42–43, 51, 53, 87, 101–2, 107, 117, 125–28, 132, 143–50, 152, 154, 157, 160–62
Melanchthon, Philip, Jr., 117
Mellerstadt, Martin, 45–46
Miltitz, Karl von, 64
Mosellanus, Petrus, xiii–xiv
Müntzer, Thomas, 104–5
Murner, Thomas, xiv
Mutian, Conrad, 38
Myconius, Friedrich, xiv

Index of Persons

Oecolampadius, Johannes, 124, 132–33
Osiander, Andreas, 127–28
Ott-Heinrich, elector of the Palatinate, 160
Paltz, Johann Jeuser von, 19, 22–23
Peter Lombard, 24, 27, 29, 33, 37, 102
Philip the Bold, duke of Burgundy, 82
Philip of Habsburg, 82
Philip, landgrave of Hesse, 105, 125, 127, 143, 154, 156
Philip, duke of Pomerania, 139

Quintilian, 39

Reinecke, Johannes, 5, 10, 11
Reuchlin, Johannes, 34, 39, 42
Rhegius, Urbanus, xiv–xv
Richard von Greiffenklau, archbishop of Trier, 94
Rörer, Georg, 149
Roth, Stephen, 121–22
Ruprecht, duke of Bavaria, 160

Sachs, Hans, 9
Schalbe, Caspar, 6
Schalbe, Heinrich, 5–6
Schappeler, Christoph, 109
Schwenckfeld, Caspar, 132
Scultetus, Hieronymus, bishop of Brandenburg, 59

Sigismund, emperor, 83
Sigismund, king of Poland, 160
Spalatin, Georg, xv, 86, 89, 112, 149
Spangenberg, Cyriakus, ix–x, xv
Staupitz, Johannes von, 21–22, 25, 36, 38, 45, 51, 55, 62–63, 70, 71, 74
Sturm, Jacob, 160

Tartaret, Pierre, 46
Tauler, Johannes, 23, 40, 60
Tetzel, Johannes, 57–61, 65–70, 72–73
Thomas Aquinas, 30, 46

Vehus, Hieronymus, 94–95

William of Ockham, 8, 24–25, 30, 37, 43–44, 108, 124
Wimpina, Konrad, 61
Wolfgang, prince of Anhalt, 154

Zwilling, Gabriel, 87–88
Zwingli, Ulrich, 123–25, 132, 133

Index of Interviews by Person Interviewed

Benedict, Georg, xii, 50–51
Bucer, Martin, xii, 73

Cochlaeus, Johann, xii, 68–69, 69–70, 70–72, 72–73, 73–74, 133–34, 137–38

Dietrich, Veit, xiii, 10

Hoffmeister, Johannes, xiii, 130–131

Luther, Martin, 8, 8–9, 9–10, 11, 12–13, 16–17, 27–28, 31–32, 32–33, 33–34, 46–48, 48–49, 49–50, 52–53, 75–76, 76–77, 77–78, 92–96, 96–97, 111–12, 112–13, 113–15, 115–16, 116–18, 135–37, 154

Mathesius, Johannes, xiii, 10–11, 15–16, 31, 46, 66–67, 67–68, 78–79, 109–11, 157–58

Melanchthon, Philip, xiii, 11, 13–14, 14–15, 26–27, 28–29, 29–30, 45–46, 51–52, 161–62

Mosellanus, Petrus, xiii-xiv, 74–75

Murner, Thomas, xiv, 50, 98–99

Myconius, Friedrich, xiv, 30–31, 65–66, 75, 155–57, 160–61

Rhegius, Urbanus, xiv-xv, 96

Spalatin, Georg, xv, 91–92, 97–98, 131–33, 138–39, 154–55, 158–59, 159–60

Spangenberg, Cyriacus, xv, 11–12, 15, 97, 131, 134–35, 157, 162

www.ingramcontent.com/pod-product-compliance
Lightning Source LLC
Chambersburg PA
CBHW020849160426
43192CB00007B/853